Quiet in the Land

Quiet in the Land

Anne Chislett

Coach House Press, Toronto

EIGHTH PRINTING

Canadian Cataloguing in Publication Data

Chislett, Anne
    Quiet in the land

A play.
ISBN 0-88910-270-8

1. Amish - Drama.   I. Title.

PS8555.H57Q53 1983   C812'.54   C83-099096-8
PR9199.3.C4945Q53 1983

Foreword

The Amish are a small religious group which originated in Germany in 1693 and came to Canada to settle the land around Kitchener, Ontario, in the 1830s. You can still see them today, with the women in their long black dresses and bonnets, driving their buggies and tilling their land with horses. The Amish-Mennonite museum in St. Jacobs, Ontario, (The Meeting Place) details the terrible history of persecution and martyrdom they have endured in order to keep their faith.

In the spring of 1980, I asked Anne Chislett if she would be interested in writing a play for the Blyth Summer Festival about the Amish in Southwestern Ontario. In December she submitted the first draft of *Quiet in the Land* which opened the 1981 season. It was a sudden and phenomenal success and was revived for a longer run in 1982. It subsequently toured to the Humanities Theatre at the University of Waterloo where it played to sold-out audiences for a week. Toronto and Montreal productions followed and, in 1982, it won the Chalmers Award for the best play presented in Toronto. Its success seemed doubly fitting because Anne Chislett with her husband James Roy had helped found the Blyth Summer Festival in 1975.

The Blyth Festival is unique in Canada in that it does only Canadian plays and concentrates especially on original works which have a special relevance to the people of rural Southwestern Ontario. The success of this and other plays is indicated by an audience growth from 3,000 in 1975 to 32,000 in 1982, an audience which is drawn primarily from the surrounding farming area to a little village of less than a thousand people. It is a demanding audience but, in *Quiet in the Land,* the care, intelligence, and the intense effort of the writer, performers, and all concerned seem to have beautifully met their expectations.

Anne made her characters so alive and their dilemmas so real that the audience was completely drawn into their world. This suggests to me that people have a great need to see themselves and the things they know and care about dealt with on the stage. And it is most exciting to find that plays written with local themes about a very particular society can reach out to people everywhere. We hope that for the audiences at Blyth and for audiences across the country, this is only the beginning.

JANET AMOS
Blyth, May, 1983

Introduction

The Amish religion developed in Germany and Switzerland from a radical movement within the Protestant Reformation of the sixteenth century. First known as Anabaptists because of the practice of adult baptism, the Amish share a common heritage with the Mennonites, Quakers, Hutterites and many other sects which hold a similar belief in the complete separation of church and state, the maintenance of a simple Christian life style and, perhaps most important within the context of our society, a total renunciation of war or killing in any form.

Because of these beliefs, from the beginning the Anabaptists came into conflict with civil and religious authority. In Europe they were bitterly persecuted by both Catholic and Protestant rulers. Their answer was to become 'the quiet in the land', which meant they withdrew to rural areas and attempted to live as simple farmers posing a threat to no one. Nevertheless, by 1800, most had been driven to migrate either to Russia, where the Czars had invited them to establish model agricultural communities, or to the New World where other dissenting religious groups had found a haven.

Unable to take either side during the American Revolution, the pacifist, or, as they term themselves, 'non-resident', Christians found themselves in trouble with both the British and Revolutionary parties. A large group of Mennonites chose to join the United Empire Loyalists in Canada where, although they were not granted the privileges accorded to the British loyalists, they were permitted to purchase land and settle in what is now Waterloo County. The success of this settlement, and the promise of freedom from conscription given by the British government led a group of Amish to migrate from Bavaria in 1823. They soon established thriving farms and, while maintaining their own language and customs, lived in harmony amid the general population.

The attempt to maintain a separate community and way of life not only brings about conflict with the larger society, but also often results in serious internal difficulties. Very early in the history of the Anabaptists, differences of opinion on specific forms of worship and lifestyle developed. Because there is no central authority, these differences led to 'splits' as each group of believers made decisions for themselves. The followers of Joseph Ammann, who became the Amish, divided from the Mennonite body in 1694 because Ammann held that stricter social discipline was necessary to guard against reabsorption into society. Shaving the beard, wearing a moustache, the use of buttons on clothing, any form of following new fashions would, in his view, mean erasing the distinction between their Christian community and the military (or simply worldly) culture surrounding them. This tendency to fragmentation over matters which seem minor to an outsider is identified by Mennonite scholars as the 'Anabaptist sickness', and has been both a strength and a weakness of the movement throughout its history.

Until the turn of the century, the Amish and Mennonites in rural Ontario were not as conspicuously different from the general population as the Old Order is today. The First World War brought their pacifism into sharp focus around the same time that rapid advances in technology, communication and transportation were creating great changes in the lifestyles of their neighbours. Added to these external threats to their traditional way of life was an increasing internal dissension due to the growth of the evangelical movement within the Mennonite (and Amish) church. Large-scale defections of young people to other denominations caused the majority to seek the renewal of their church through the adoption of Protestant revivalist models, including Sunday schools, missionary societies, revival meetings and organised charitable works. For the minority who became the Old Order, the evangelical movement, with its emphasis on personal salvation and personal ethics, threatened the fabric of the total community which they continued to see as the centre of the Christian life. The dropping of many of the barriers between themselves and the 'proud and worldly', especially the use of English as opposed to the German language, that went hand in hand with the 'reawakening' of the church, proved to be too great a compromise for those who wished to remain a 'separate and peculiar' people.

The major source of Quiet in the Land, and one which I recommend to any seeking further knowledge of the Amish and Mennonite history, is Mennonites in Canada: The History of a Separate People in two volumes by Frank H. Epp, published by Macmillan of Canada, Toronto.

ANNE CHISLETT
Victoria, May, 1983

Quiet in the Land

Quiet in the Land was first performed at the Blyth Summer Festival on July 3rd, 1981 with the following cast.

CHRISTY BAUMAN	David Fox
JAKE BAUMAN	Keith Thomas
HANNAH BAUMAN	Beth Amos
ZEPP BRUBACHER	Sam Robinson
LYDIE BRUBACHER	Janet Amos
KATIE BRUBACHER	Kate Trotter
MARTHA BRUBACHER	Denise Kennedy
NANCY BRUBACHER	Susie Walsh
MENNO MILLER	William Dunlop
BISHOP ELI FREY	Dean Hawes
MR. O'ROURKE	Dean Hawes
PADDY O'ROURKE	Graham McPherson
RECRUITMENT OFFICER	Graham McPherson
CHILDREN	Peter Cook, Rachel Thompson, Deanna Bearrs
DIRECTOR	Guy Sprung
SET DESIGNER	John Ferguson
COSTUME DESIGNER	Kerry Hackett
LIGHTING DESIGNER	Louise Guinand
STAGE MANAGER	Sarah Wakely

The Characters

CHRISTY (Christian) BAUMAN, an Amish farmer aged between 40-45
YOCK (Jacob) BAUMAN, Christy's son, aged 18-22
HANNAH BAUMAN, Christy's mother, aged 60-70
ZEPP (Joseph) BRUBACHER, an Amish farmer, the deacon of the congregation, same age as Christy
LYDIA (Lydie) BRUBACHER, Zepp's wife, aged around 40
KATIE BRUBACHER, Zepp's oldest daughter, about 18
MARTHA BRUBACHER, Zepp's middle daughter, about 16
NANCY BRUBACHER, Zepp's youngest daughter, about 11
MENNO MILLER, a friend of Yock's, about the same age
LEVI MILLER (extra), Menno's father, aged 40-60
ESTHER MILLER (extra), Menno's mother, aged 40-60
PADAH (Peter) MILLER (extra), Menno's younger brother, aged 10-15
MR. O'ROURKE, an Irish farmer and neighbour, aged 40
PADDY O'ROURKE, Mr. O'Rourke's son, the same age as Yock
BISHOP ELI FREY, a visiting bishop from Ohio, with 'oversight' of this congregation
other children and extras as available
RECRUITING OFFICER

The play takes place in a farming area near Kitchener, Ontario
Act One, 1917
Act Two, 1918

Act I, scene i
The exterior of the Brubacher house
Early fall, 1917

Inside the BRUBACHER house, which we might only glimpse through windows, the Sunday meeting of an old order Amish congregation is entering its fourth hour.

Benches have been set up so that the women are seated on one side, the men on the other, in order of age. They could be in separate rooms. Between them is a small preaching table with a jug of water, a Bible and another old book.

Outside, a simple table is set against the wall of the house. On it are covered baskets of foods which can be eaten without cutlery.

The music, which might begin as pre-curtain music, is a hymn from the Ausband, the old order hymn book, sung by the congregation in unison. (No harmony or accompaniment is permitted.) The hymn should be led by the 'vorsinger' who controls the melody by singing the first note of each verse alone. The singing fades out under the BISHOP's sermon but may return during or after the baptism.

As the lights come up, BISHOP ELI FREY is giving his sermon. The children are beginning to grow restless and a few adults might be seen to nod. (The preaching style is extremely plain, no gestures, no vocal flourishes.)

BISHOP: ... But the world won't leave us alone. And now this country has declared its Military Service Act. That means they will try to make us fight in their sinful war. I'm going to read to you what Menno Simons said about that four hundred years ago. [*He picks up a book and fumbles for the page.*] 'I tell you the truth in Christ, those who are baptized according to the word of the Lord have no weapons except patience, love, silence and God's word. The weapons of our warfare are not weapons with which cities may be destroyed and human blood shed in torrents like water. Love is the only weapon a Christian can know, even if we be torn into a thousand pieces and if as many false witnesses rise up against us as there are spears of grass in the fields, and grains of sand on the seashore.'

[*The congregation stirs, thinking he is finished.* ZEPP *rises and takes the jug of water.*]

BISHOP: [*Continuing*] You see, our people [*He sees* ZEPP *and glances at his watch.*] Oh ... Amen.

ZEPP: Those to be baptized.

[MENNO MILLER *and* KATIE BRUBACHER *leave their places and kneel before the* BISHOP.]

BISHOP: Wherefore come ye out from among them, and be ye separate and touch not the unclean thing and I will receive you, saith the Lord.

[YOCK BAUMAN *and* PADDY O'ROURKE *approach the house.* PADDY *is limping slightly. Both could be a bit muddy.* YOCK *sneaks a glance in the window, but motions* PADDY *away when he tries to look.* YOCK *gives him a cookie to distract him.*]

[*While* YOCK *and* PADDY *have their scene in front of the house, inside the* BISHOP *baptises* MENNO *and* KATE. *We might hear his words as background or just the hymn being sung softly.* ZEPP *and* LYDIE *assist in the baptism.*]

YOCK: [*He speaks with some hesitancy, because he has not spoken English since he left school at age 14.*] The meeting is almost over, if you ...

PADDY: You're not going to be in trouble, are you?

YOCK: Do not worry. I was going to say Menno will be out. With two horses ...

PADDY: Nah, she's in over her running boards. It's going to take Dad and the team.

YOCK: I guess you are in trouble, too?

PADDY: Dad thinks more of that car than he does of me for sure. If she's scratched bad, I won't bother waiting to get called up.

YOCK: You would join the army?

PADDY: We'll all have to soon. Anyways, I'm looking forward to getting a crack at those German bastards. Oh ... I'm sorry. I never think of you as being ... I mean, at school, you seemed just like the rest of us.

YOCK: We are not German. We just speak it.

[*Inside the house the final verse of the hymn has begun. A child begins to cry.* HANNAH BAUMAN *takes the child outside to gently wipe her nose and quiet her.* HANNAH *notices* PADDY *with obvious disapproval.*]

PADDY: Oh. [*He sees* HANNAH.] Well, I better be going. Thanks for trying.

YOCK: It is all right.

PADDY: I hope you didn't strain your horse or nothing.

[PADDY *exits with a wave.*]

HANNAH: Who was that?

YOCK: [*With no accent*] Paddy O'Rourke. You know, that farm next to Miller's.

HANNAH: Did I hear you speaking that English?

YOCK: He doesn't speak German, Gros mutti.

HANNAH: [*Shaking her head*] On top of missing the meeting. Your poor doddy will ...

[HANNAH *breaks off as the young people,* KATE, MENNO, MARTHA, NANCY *and assorted children spill out of the house.* MENNO *and* KATE *are the centre of attention.* KATE *is swinging her bonnet in one hand. All other girls have theirs on.*]

MARTHA: [*Hugging* KATE] I suppose you feel all grown up.

KATE: I feel wet.

[KATE *pushes back her covering and attempts to fluff her hair a little.*]

NANCY: Mom said you'd feel closer to Jesus.

MENNO: Jah, it felt like He was right beside us, didn't it, Katie?

[KATE *smiles, but doesn't answer.*]

YOCK: You'll be a preacher yet.

MENNO: You weren't even there, were you?

MARTHA: I guess he was shamed at not getting baptised himself.

YOCK: I was not.

KATE: [*At the same time*] Martha, be quiet.

[LYDIE *and* ESTHER *come out of the house.* LYDIE *goes to* KATE *and hugs her. She gives her a new Bible.* ESTHER *gives one to* MENNO, *who is embarrassed.* HANNAH *comes out and goes to* KATE.]

HANNAH: Be welcome as a sister in the church, Katie. Why, child, your mother didn't do a very good job of putting your covering back on.

[HANNAH *pulls* KATE'S *covering forward over her hair, and tightens the bow under her chin.*]

KATE: Thank you, Hannah. [*Grimacing*]

HANNAH: You're a real little Amish woman now.

[LYDIE, HANNAH *and* ESTHER *go up to the table to lay out food.*]

YOCK: [*As soon as they have turned away*] Real little Amish woman!

KATE: Better than being a real little Amish child!

MARTHA: Katie can start courting now.

YOCK: That why you got baptised?

[KATE *flounces away angrily, followed by other girls. They begin a quiet game or conversation.*]

MENNO: [*To* YOCK] What are you being so smart for?

YOCK: What did you knuckle under for?

MENNO: What?

YOCK: Why did you join the church?

MENNO: God wanted me to.

YOCK: Your Pa, you mean.

MENNO: Well, jah, him too. But I prayed about it ... and ...

YOCK: Jah?

MENNO: It's like you want to fly, you're that happy.

[ESTHER *goes inside for a jug of water perhaps.*]

YOCK: You mean, like if Katie let you take her home from singing?

MENNO: [*Blushing*] Aw, Yock. [*He looks down,* YOCK *grins*]

HANNAH: [*To* LYDIE] You must be pleased with your girl.

LYDIE: Makes me feel old. [*Trying not to sound proud*]

HANNAH: Wait till you're a gros-mutti.

LYDIE: Ach, Katie's too young to think on boys.

YOCK: You never even get the nerve to ask her, do you?

MARTHA: [*Who can see the boys from where she's standing*] Yock's looking at you, Katie.

KATE: [*Refusing to turn around*] Let him!

MARTHA: [*Teasing her*] Just the way he looks at Moira O'Rourke.

KATE: [*Flaring*] He can't look at her. She's not Christian.

MENNO: [*Finally coming up with a response*] I don't see you asking her either.

YOCK: Maybe I don't want to.

MENNO: Huh!

MARTHA: Is Menno looking at me?

KATE: Yock Bauman thinks he's so good.

HANNAH: [*Drawing* LYDIE'*s attention to the boys staring at the girls*] There's boys thinking on her, Lydie.

LYDIE: Ach, Menno's so doppich and Yock's not even baptised yet.

HANNAH: [*Hurt*] It's not that he weren't brought up right.

LYDIE: [*Realizing that she has put her foot in her mouth*] Oh, Hannah, I didn't mean —

HANNAH: I did my best for him, just like I promised his poor dying mutti.

LYDIE: I know, I know.

[*The* MEN *come out of the house.*]

[*The* BISHOP *and* ZEPP *go to the table.* LEVI *goes to* MENNO. CHRISTY *is a step or two behind.*]

BISHOP: How are you, Hannah?

HANNAH: Growing old, Eli.

LEVI: [*Clapping* MENNO *on the back*] You eat with the men now, son.

[LEVI *leads* MENNO *away from* YOCK *to the table.* ESTHER *has returned and happily gives him something to eat.*]

CHRISTY: [*Crossing to* YOCK] You didn't even have the courage to show your face?

YOCK: I was on my way, Pa, but —

CHRISTY: Haven't you shamed me enough?

[YOCK *doesn't answer.* CHRISTY *turns back to the table where the men are eating.*]

CHRISTY: Is there any left, or did Lydie eat it all?

LYDIE: Blame Zepp, he didn't give me time for breakfast.

ZEPP: Ach, you were too jumpy to think about food.

BISHOP: It's not every day your daughter joins the church.

LYDIE: Maybe not, but it's more often than I miss a meal.

[ALL laugh. MENNO *returns to* YOCK.]

LEVI: We better get a move on, Esther.

ESTHER: Oh, jah.

LEVI: We got relatives coming from all over.

HANNAH: I know, we been helping Esther shine tinware all week.

[LEVI *shakes hands with the* BISHOP *during this exchange, and he and* ESTHER *head off.*]

LEVI: You won't be long, Menno?

MENNO: No, Pa.

[CHRISTY, ZEPP *and the* BISHOP *have moved away from the table.*]

CHRISTY: [*To the* BISHOP] I judged my son too young to join.

BISHOP: [*Uncomfortable with what he knows is a lie*] I'm sure you were wise, Christy.

ZEPP: Oh, jah, it'll be Yock's turn next year.

[YOCK *and* MENNO *overhear this.* YOCK *toes the ground.*]

CHRISTY: So what's all the news from Ohio?

BISHOP: Nothing but war now the Americans are in it. They're putting pressure on our boys. I'm afraid this conscription up here is going to be trouble for you, too.

CHRISTY: I got Yock a farm deferment, simple as [*snaps fingers*].

BISHOP: The government can take that away just as simple.

CHRISTY: They need farmers as much as soldiers. Why, they're buying the crops before the seed's even sown.

[BISHOP *and* MEN *walk upstage.*]

YOCK: [*To* MENNO] I couldn't just say the words, not when I don't believe them.

MENNO: What don't you —

YOCK: [*Rushing on*] That would have been blasphemy. Pa wouldn't have wanted that, would he?

MENNO: I don't guess. [*Pause*] What did he say?

YOCK: That I'd either join next year or get out.

MENNO: But when you told him, about not believing?

YOCK: You think I'm crazy?

MENNO: He could have explained whatever ... to you ...

YOCK: Sure! 'Pa, tell me why I have to go to hell if I don't agree with every stupid rule the elders make up.' You know what would have happened. Same thing always happens.

MENNO: Jah.

YOCK: Come on. I'm starved.

[YOCK *moves to the table where the young people are now having their turn to eat.* MENNO *stays where he is.* BISHOP *and* MEN *turn downstage.*]

BISHOP: You'd better know, the Canadians almost didn't let me cross the border this time. They wanted to know if I was going to preach against the war. 'What else can a Christian do?' I asked.

ZEPP: Jah.

BISHOP: If you do run into trouble and I'm not around, this man might be of some help.

[*The* BISHOP *gives* ZEPP *a piece of paper.* CHRISTY *reads over his shoulder.*]

CHRISTY: Coffman? He Amish?

BISHOP: Mennonite. [*Seeing* CHRISTY's *reaction*] But not reformed.

ZEPP: Jah, well.

[MENNO *crosses to the men and waits to be noticed.*]

CHRISTY: We'll be fine, as long as we mind our own business.

BISHOP: [*Seeing* MENNO] Our newest brother.

CHRISTY: Welcome to the church, Menno.

MENNO: Thank you. [*Pause*] Bishop Eli, if you're not busy... could I ...

BISHOP: Jah, Menno?

ZEPP: [*Seeing* MENNO *wants to talk alone*] Want to give me a hand with the table now, Christy?

CHRISTY: [*A bit surprised*] Sure.

[*The* YOUNG PEOPLE *have moved away from the table.* LYDIE *and* HANNAH *are packing things away.* ZEPP *and* CHRISTY *move the table inside the house.*]

MENNO: Some of the boys ... you know ... they got a lot of questions.

BISHOP: Can't your elders deal with them?

MENNO: Jah. [*Pause*]

BISHOP: Aren't their answers good enough for you?

MENNO: Oh, jah, sure. [*Gathering courage*] They'd be good enough if we got any.

BISHOP: What's that supposed to mean?

MENNO: Mostly the elders just tell us to obey and leave the worry to them.

BISHOP: I see.

MENNO: I felt ... when you were pouring the water ... that there was something God wanted me to do.

BISHOP: Everyone feels that when they're being baptised.

[LYDIE *and* ZEPP *move small things inside the house.* HANNAH *and* CHRISTY *are standing together.*]

MENNO: I don't mean I think I'm special or anything.

HANNAH: [*Watching* MENNO *and the* BISHOP] It's not like Menno to put himself forward.

CHRISTY: No, it isn't.

[*By this time everyone on stage has become aware that* MENNO *is talking to the* BISHOP. *All are staring, a few whispering.*]

HANNAH: That whole family are slow as sheep most times.

KATE: [*To* YOCK] What do you think Menno's doing?

YOCK: I dunno. Listen, Katie?

KATE: Jah?

YOCK: You need a ride to singing tonight? I go right past your house.

KATE: [*Uncertain*] Oh ... well ...

YOCK: We can take Martha ... if you want.

KATE: Jah, all right.

YOCK: I'll give you a ride home, too.

KATE: Oh ... but ...

[The BISHOP *leads* MENNO *back toward* ZEPP.]

BISHOP: [*So that all can hear*] Menno is asking permission to start a young people's group.

[CHRISTY *takes a step toward the* BISHOP.]

ZEPP: A Sunday school?

[ZEPP *and* CHRISTY *look at each other, not pleased. They both look at* MENNO, *who is suffering the tortures of the damned.*]

HANNAH: [*To* LYDIE] That was one of the things my man split with Mornington over.

BISHOP: Menno thinks the young people will attend.

MENNO: If there was someone to lead.

BISHOP: You're the one to lead.

MENNO: [*Appalled*] Oh, no, not me. I can't put two words together.

BISHOP: If the Lord is guiding you, He'll give you the words. You have my blessing, Menno.

MENNO: Thank you, Bishop Eli.

[MENNO *escapes to where* YOCK *is standing.*]

CHRISTY: Bishop Eli ...

[ZEPP *puts a hand on his arm and takes over the conversation.*]

ZEPP: That's the kind of decision the membership sometimes like to talk over, Eli.

BISHOP: Jah, Zepp, but you are the last congregation to start one.

CHRISTY: Because when my father was Bishop, he wouldn't allow it. He said it was aping the worldly churches.

BISHOP: Now, they'll just be getting together a few afternoons to study the Bible.

CHRISTY: I know, but look what just happened in Hay Township.

BISHOP: What did you hear about that?

ZEPP: Well, we heard you baptised some boys that Bishop Shantz turned down. Some that wouldn't grow beards and refused to wear the plain coat.

BISHOP: There would have been another split else.

CHRISTY: Splitting's not the worst thing. Not standing fast in the ways of our fathers, that's worse.

BISHOP: I was satisfied the ones in Hay had God in their hearts, whatever was on their backs.

ZEPP: Jah, Eli, except they say now you can't tell a Hay Amish from a Methodist.

CHRISTY: You see, they start deciding what scripture means for themselves ... and they don't ... they haven't lived long enough, I suppose I mean.

BISHOP: It's a different world than when we were boys, you know. We're losing a lot of our young people these days.

CHRISTY: Not from this church.

BISHOP: When your father was Bishop, he would have been baptising ten or twelve a year. How many today?

[CHRISTY *is silent.*]

ZEPP: Well, if you're in favour, Eli ...

BISHOP: I am. And, Deacon, it'll be up to you to keep an eye on how they get on.

ZEPP: Jah. Are you coming to dinner with us?

BISHOP: I promised I'd spend some time in East Zorra. I'll just say

David Fox (Christy), Sam Robinson (Zepp) and Dean Hawes (Bishop).

goodbye to Hannah and be on my way.

[BISHOP *shakes hands with* CHRISTY *and* ZEPP *and crosses to exchange a few words with the women.*]

[*When they see the end of the confrontation, the young people relax.* KATE *and* MARTHA *cross to* MENNO *and* YOCK.]

KATE: I want to tell you, Menno, I think that was brave of you.

MENNO: Oh, no ... I ... it ...

YOCK: More church!

[*The* BISHOP *acknowledges the young people as he passes. He shakes hands with* MENNO *and exits.*]

MENNO: [*A sudden surge of courage*] Katie, could I offer you a ride to singing tonight?

KATE: Oh, Yock already asked us.

MENNO: Oh.

MARTHA: We'll see you there.

[*The* GIRLS *go back to the children.*]

[MENNO *looks reproachfully at* YOCK, *who grins.*]

LYDIE: You folks coming to Yoder's for dinner?

CHRISTY: Jah, though the way young Susan's been dressing, I don't see how Dan can have enough money left over to feed us.

LYDIE: She told Martha she was making a new dress ... yellow. [*Giggles*]

HANNAH: The Devil's in that girl's needle for sure.

ZEPP: Oh, we could use a bit of colour, maybe.

CHRISTY: At least you made Kate let her skirts down some.

LYDIE: Now, don't you go picking on Kate, Christy Bauman, just 'cause she got baptised and your ...

ZEPP: [*Cutting her off*] 'Bout ready to go, Lydie?

LYDIE: I'll get the children.

[LYDIE *begins to round up her girls.*]

HANNAH: You know Katie is a good girl, Christy.

CHRISTY: Jah, I do. [*Slight pause*] It's the worry makes me mean, Zepp.

ZEPP: I don't think we've too much to worry about.

CHRISTY: Lately, I look around ... I see us letting the world in one little step at a time. But that Sunday school, that's a big step.

ZEPP: Menno's not the sort to cause trouble.

CHRISTY: He's quiet enough, I'll grant you that.

ZEPP: And I seem to recall just last week you were complaining that the baptism class could hardly read High German. The meetings will give 'em a chance to practise.

CHRISTY: That's what they thought over in Hay, and before anyone knew it, German was out the window and they were talking about what was wrong with their parents ... in English!

HANNAH: Like Yock this morning!

CHRISTY: [*Startled*] What, mutti?

HANNAH: He was talking with that Canadian boy. Talking English.

CHRISTY: [*Calling*] Yock, come over here.

YOCK: Jah, Pa? [*Crosses to him*]

CHRISTY: What's all this about this morning?

YOCK: [*Glancing at* HANNAH] Pa, Paddy O'Rourke tried to pass me in that automobile of his and my horse reared and Paddy ended up in Jantzi's swamp.

ZEPP: I guess them automobiles scare easy.

YOCK: I couldn't just leave him there, Pa.

ZEPP: Now there's something about that in the Bible, isn't there?

CHRISTY: You don't need to remind me.

HANNAH: The Lord may have pulled a mule out of a bog on the Sabbath, but you can be sure he did it in Christian speech.

CHRISTY: [*Amused in spite of himself*] Jah, well … [*With resolve*] Yock, I spoke too soon, before.

[ZEPP *covers a grin and walks toward* MENNO.]

YOCK: I … it doesn't matter …

[*Pause*]

CHRISTY: Well, we're keeping the Yoders waiting.

YOCK: Oh … Menno asked me to eat with them, if that's all right.

CHRISTY: Sure.

[YOCK *heads back to* MENNO.]

LYDIE: [*Off*] What's keeping you folks?

HANNAH: [*Hurrying off*] Poor Lydie, she must be starving.

ZEPP: Just one thing, Menno … about that Bible group. If the Lord gives you the words, like the Bishop said, make sure you hear him in High German.

MENNO: [*Catching on*] Oh, jah … I will.

YOCK: Ready?

[YOCK *exits with* MENNO.]

MENNO: [*As they go*] I don't know why I should feed you. Not after you beating me out with Katie.

CHRISTY: [*Looking after the boys*] Do you really think I'm worrying too much?

ZEPP: Sometimes all you can do is love 'em and pray they find their own way.

CHRISTY: But what will I do if he doesn't join next year?

ZEPP: Trust in the Lord, and then, as Lydie says, we'll be all right … as long as nothing goes wrong.

[*Blackout*]

scene ii
The BAUMAN kitchen and exterior
The BRUBACHER kitchen
A few days later

Both kitchens are scrubbed and neat. The only decorations are functional, except for potted herbs or flowers. HANNAH's kitchen should be plainer than LYDIE's.

HANNAH is sitting in her kitchen mending or darning.

YOCK is outside fixing a harness.

In the Brubacher kitchen, LYDIE and KATE are putting the last supper things away. ZEPP's place is still set.

KATE: Sure not many dishes when there's just the two of us.

LYDIE: I don't know what's keeping your doddy, but I was that glad not to see him.

KATE: Mom!

LYDIE: Because I'm so far behind, I mean.

KATE: You never told me where you were all afternoon?

LYDIE: Oh, the most terrible thing happened. [*Giggles*]

KATE: What?

LYDIE: Well, I ... no, you get the clothes off the line, I'll clean up the wash house ... and I'll tell you when your father gets home.

[*They exit.*]

CHRISTY: [*Looking up from his Bible to share a passage with* HANNAH] 'With the ancient is wisdom and in length of days is understanding.'

HANNAH: Yah, and don't you forget it.

[ZEPP *enters the Bauman yard and approaches the door.*]

[YOCK *puts down his work and opens the door.*]

YOCK: Pa, Zepp's here.

CHRISTY: Jah? [*He comes to the doorway.*]

ZEPP: I'm on my way back from town, I brought your mail.

[ZEPP *gives* CHRISTY *a card.*]

CHRISTY: That's neighbourly.

ZEPP: Read it and see if you still think so.

[CHRISTY *reads the card. He speaks the English words with difficulty.*]

CHRISTY: 'National Service.' This the government?

ZEPP: [*Nods*] One for Yock too. [*Gives the card to* YOCK.]

CHRISTY: You better sit down.

[CHRISTY *and* ZEPP *go in, followed by* YOCK.]

HANNAH: Zepp, would you like some coffee?

ZEPP: I had some at Miller's, thanks, Hannah.

CHRISTY: You been making the rounds with these?

ZEPP: Not yet. I sent young Menno to see if the Bishop is still in East Zorra.

CHRISTY: We don't need Eli Frey to tell us to have nothing to do with the army. Put these in the stove, Yock.

ZEPP: Now, hold on ...

YOCK: This isn't conscription, Pa.

ZEPP: No?

YOCK: They want us to register, that's all. Every Canadian male between 16 and 65 has got to fill one out and return it.

CHRISTY: Not us.

YOCK: But it's the law.

CHRISTY: Put them in the stove.

[YOCK *takes his card and* CHRISTY's *and throws them in the stove.*]

ZEPP: I expect the government has plenty more.

CHRISTY: Good. We won't need kindling all winter.

[MENNO *knocks at the door.* YOCK *opens it.*]

MENNO: Is the deacon here?

ZEPP: You back from East Zorra already?

MENNO: No ... [*Remembering manners*] Evening, Christy, Hannah. [*To* ZEPP] I just got as far as the crossroads and I ran into Dave Schultz from Hay Township.

ZEPP: Jah?

MENNO: He said some government men came after Bishop Eli. They took him away.

HANNAH: Took him where?

MENNO: Dave didn't know.

YOCK: Oh, don't worry, Gros Mutti, they probably just deported him.

CHRISTY: What would you know about it?

YOCK: They been deporting enemy aliens lately. There's been a lot of stories in the paper, almost every day...

CHRISTY: [*Sharply*] What paper?

YOCK: [*Caught out*] I just glanced at one in the village.

CHRISTY: You just glanced at a lot of stories almost every day?

YOCK: I can't help wanting to know what's going on, Pa.

CHRISTY: There is nothing in any English paper of any concern to you. But you don't have to make matters worse by lying.

YOCK: I'm sorry.

CHRISTY: 'Evil has many tools, but a lie is the handle that fits them all.' You finish fixing that harness?

YOCK: Not yet.

CHRISTY: Better get it done.

[YOCK *and* MENNO *exit.*]

HANNAH: Deported? What does that mean?

CHRISTY: We won't see him again while the war lasts.

HANNAH: 'What the Lord doeth is well done.'

ZEPP: What do you mean, Hannah?

HANNAH: I'd be the last to wish Eli Frey any harm, Zepp, but it'll be better for all of us if the Lord keeps him stuck in Ohio.

CHRISTY: Mutti, the Lord did not start a war so we would have to make our own bishop.

ZEPP: [*Anxious to avoid this conversation*] Well, Lydie's going to be wondering what's happened to me.

CHRISTY: I'll walk you to the fence.

[ZEPP *nods at* HANNAH *and puts on his hat.* KATE *and* LYDIE *enter their kitchen with baskets of laundry and begin folding clothes, linen, etc.* ZEPP *and* CHRISTY *stroll to the exit.*]

CHRISTY: Without a bishop, all this army business will be on your shoulders.

ZEPP: I guess.

CHRISTY: It won't be easy for you.

ZEPP: No.

CHRISTY: I'm wondering if you should call a meeting?

ZEPP: Well ...

[CHRISTY *and* ZEPP *clear.*]

KATE: [*Holding up a nightshirt of Zepp's that's full of holes.*] Time to make rags of this, Mom?

LYDIE: Ach, no. Your doddy likes a breeze.

[KATE *takes nightshirt and a few other items to her treadle sewing machine, or she can hand sew.*]

[*On another part of the stage,* YOCK *and* MENNO *are working on the harness.*]

YOCK: Sometimes I think the army wouldn't be too bad.

MENNO: Yock, it's full of heathen!

YOCK: Maybe I'd be right at home.

MENNO: You're just saying that.

YOCK: Have you been to town lately? You see how they stare?

MENNO: Jah.

YOCK: One woman yelled 'shirker,' right in my face.

MENNO: High people don't know any better. Listen, we're having our first Bible meeting Sunday ... and there's more than you concerned about the war, you know.

YOCK: Pa'd have a fit.

MENNO: We could talk it out.

YOCK: 'Course I couldn't be in more trouble than I am now.

MENNO: Jah.

YOCK: [*Drops harness in some horseplay and takes off,* MENNO *in pursuit*] Jah!

[ZEPP *enters his own house, hangs up his coat and hat and looks for pen and paper.*]

[CHRISTY *might stand on his step in thought.*]

LYDIE: What kept you, Zepp?

ZEPP: You didn't wait supper, did you?

LYDIE: Ach, no, yours is in the oven.

ZEPP: Maybe later.

[*He finds pen and paper and sits down to write a letter. It is a laborious undertaking.*]

[CHRISTY *enters his house where* HANNAH *is eagerly awaiting him.*]

HANNAH: Son, I've always known you were meant to look after your doddy's church.

CHRISTY: You shouldn't say that, mutti.

HANNAH: It's not pride, son. It's need. Did you see what Sally Yost put up to her windows? Curtains!

CHRISTY: Zepp said they're real plain ones.

HANNAH: Blinds were good enough for her mother.

CHRISTY: Rube Meyer buying that gas engine bothers me more. Still, they're common as dirt now. So, maybe we reconsider. Maybe they're not pride anymore.

HANNAH: Your doddy had a rule. If you're going to make a mistake, make it on the side you're sure is safe.

CHRISTY: Jah. [*He throws a log into the stove and notices that the woodbox is nearly empty.*] I can't say I'd be sorry if we decide to elect another bishop.

[CHRISTY *exits.* ZEPP *is having trouble with his letter.* KATE *is still sewing.* LYDIE *is folding laundry.*]

LYDIE: I talked to the Devil today. Only it wasn't the Devil at all. It was Mrs. O'Rourke's sister from Kitchener.

ZEPP: Why did you think Mrs. O'Rourke's sister was the Devil?

LYDIE: Because Hannah said only the Devil could make himself small enough to get through the wire.

KATE: What wire?

LYDIE: We're supposed to visit the sick, aren't we? Even if they're not Amish?

KATE: Who's sick?

LYDIE: I took the butter and eggs to the store this morning, and there's Mr. O'Rourke trying to do his shopping from a list. Only he couldn't make out what was wrote. So, I thought, here's a chance to be neighbourly, [*Pointedly, to* ZEPP] like we're supposed to be.

KATE: Jah?

LYDIE: So he tells me Mrs. O'Rourke has a sick head. Well, as soon as I got home, I made up a batch of chamomile and ·sage and ran right over.

ZEPP: Consequences? [*Trying to write foreign word*]

LYDIE: What's that?

ZEPP: What the government is going to do to us if I don't get this letter written.

LYDIE: Oh. Anyway, while I was waiting for the kettle to boil –

KATE: Mom, you went into their house?

LYDIE: Well, she wouldn't know how to brew up my herbs.

ZEPP: Same as tea.

LYDIE: So, this box on the wall goes Bringggg.

KATE: The O'Rourkes got a telephone?

LYDIE: One of the first in the township.

ZEPP: You talked on it?

LYDIE: Oh, no. [*She returns to active folding for a beat*] It wasn't theirs. 'Whoever it is, it's not us they be wanting,' she said. 'Ach, I'm glad,' I said. 'It is the Devil and I'm glad it's not you he wanting be.' My English is getting better, isn't it, Kate?

ZEPP: It'll soon be good enough to explain how to boil water.

LYDIE: Well, 'Faith and begorrah,' she said. 'What makes you think it's the Devil?' So I told her about Hannah and she laughed till her head hurt too much. [*She folds an article of clothing*] Then, when we were drinking our brew...

KATE: Mom!

LYDIE: I had to stay, Katie! She might have thought I was trying to poison her if I just brewed it up and walked out again.

ZEPP: Conscience? Does that start with a C or a K?

LYDIE: You know I can't spell English.

KATE: C.

ZEPP: Then how did you read O'Rourke's list?

LYDIE: Ach, I don't need the words to know the groceries.

Anyway, this thing went again. Only this time, it went Bring-Bring. And she said to me, 'You pick up it.' Now, Zepp, I couldn't have a Catholic thinking the Amish are afraid of the Devil, could I? [*With a touch of chagrin*] Only it wasn't the Devil at all. It was her sister from Kitchener.

[LYDIE *exits with laundry.*]

[CHRISTY *enters with an armload of wood which he dumps in the woodbox.*]

CHRISTY: Suppose I nominate Zepp? He's already deacon.

HANNAH: Zepp has a good heart, but it's a misguided love that lets us fall into sin. No, son, you are the only man strong enough to put us to rights. Zepp can nominate you. Then nobody else will stand.

CHRISTY: Shouldn't the Lord have a choice, Mutti?

HANNAH: If the Lord had wanted a choice, He would have given us one.

CHRISTY: 'Seekest thou great things for thyself, seek them not.'

HANNAH: For the church, Christy... not for yourself.

[CHRISTY *picks up his Bible and begins to read.*]

[LYDIE *returns to her kitchen.*]

LYDIE: The girls are awful late, Zepp.

ZEPP: Oh, Dan'll send them home before it gets dark.

LYDIE: Who are you writing to?

ZEPP: Bishop Coffman.

LYDIE: What happened to Bishop Frey?

ZEPP: The government got him.

LYDIE: Oh.

KATE: [*Upset*] Bishop Eli?

ZEPP: Now, hush, Eli is used to trouble, he'll be all right.

LYDIE: Can't you write in German?

Keith Thomas (Yock).

ZEPP: You'd think he'd still know German? He's a Mennonite.

LYDIE: He'd have to. The Bible's wrote in it.

ZEPP: Jah. [*He crumples up his letter.*]

LYDIE: Of course, the post office wouldn't send it.

ZEPP: Jah. [*He straightens out the letter.*]

[LYDIE *goes to the window to look for her children.* YOCK *enters* CHRISTY's *with an armload of wood.*]

YOCK: [*Seeing box filled*] You didn't have to, Pa.

CHRISTY: No, I could let your grosmutti freeze to death.

YOCK: I been working all day.

HANNAH: Ach, you young ones. You don't know what work is. You'll have twice as much when your doddy's bishop.

YOCK: What?

CHRISTY: Mutti ...

HANNAH: He won't have time for choring.

YOCK: Are you going to be bishop?

CHRISTY: I might be ... if I'm called.

HANNAH: Yock, you'll have to say you've decided to join the church next year for sure.

YOCK: No ... I mean ... I can't ... Grosmutti.

CHRISTY: Why can't you?

HANNAH: A bishop's son is expected to set an example.

YOCK: That's not a good enough reason ... I'm just not sure ...

CHRISTY: [*With temper*] What aren't you sure about? [*No response*] What's wrong with you?

YOCK: Nothing. [*He starts to exit.*]

CHRISTY: Where are you going?

YOCK: I'm not finished in the barn.

[CHRISTY *shrugs.* YOCK *exits.*]

CHRISTY: What am I going to do with him, Mutti?

HANNAH: Ach, you forget how much trouble you were.

CHRISTY: Me?

HANNAH: Why, before you started courting Sarah, your doddy used to worry himself ...

[HANNAH *suddenly gets an idea and jumps up and puts on her bonnet.*]

CHRISTY: What are you doing?

HANNAH: I want to see Lydie before it gets dark.

CHRISTY: What for?

HANNAH: Something to do with the understanding of the ancient.

[HANNAH *exits.*]

LYDIE: [*Looking up from her task*] Christy shouldn't be made bishop, Zepp.

ZEPP: [*Giving her full attention*] Who said anything about Christy being bishop?

LYDIE: He wants it too much.

ZEPP: Hmmmmm.

[ZEPP *returns to his letter.*]

[LYDIE *crosses to the window.*]

ZEPP: The girls will be fine.

LYDIE: One of them tele-things would be right handy, you know.

ZEPP: No, Lydie.

LYDIE: But if it's not the Devil ...?

ZEPP: It's the wires. They'd join us with the high people. 'Be ye not yoked unequally with unbelievers.'

[LYDIE *looks out the window again.* ZEPP *returns to his letter.*]

LYDIE: But think of the trouble you'd save. You wouldn't have to spell that letter out, and Hannah wouldn't have to climb over that stile.

ZEPP: What? [*Hides letter*]

LYDIE: She's cutting through the garden right now. [*Goes to the door and calls to her*] Hannah, what brings you over?

HANNAH: [*Still outside*] Finished your canning?

LYDIE: Except that I might get a few more tomatoes.

HANNAH: There'll be frost soon. I can feel it in my bones. Where are your girls?

LYDIE: Martha and Nancy are over at Yoders.

[HANNAH *enters.*]

HANNAH: There's Katie. She's the one I want.

LYDIE: Oh?

HANNAH: I want you to hire her out to me till after harvest.

KATE: Oh, Mutti, can I?

LYDIE: Ach, I couldn't do without her.

HANNAH: But you just said you're all done.

LYDIE: Zepp would miss her too much.

KATE: Doddy, please.

HANNAH: Ach, Zepp, we're just two steps and a hop.

LYDIE: Barbara Weber is more experienced.

HANNAH: That one! Her covering was so small last Sunday, I had to look twice to see if she was wearing one. You should talk to her, Zepp. No, I've my heart set on Kate.

KATE: I know how to work, Doddy.

LYDIE: Zepp?

KATE: Doddy?

HANNAH: I'm just too old and tired to manage harvest on my own.

[MARTHA *and* NANCY *come into the room in tears.* O'ROURKE *is behind them. He hesitates in the open doorway and knocks.*]

LYDIE: Vat is —

HANNAH: Oh, child, what happened to you?

O'ROURKE: Uh ... I'm ... Jimmy, my youngest, and some of the buckos ganged up on them.

NANCY: They threw stones at us.

O'ROURKE: I want you to know, they caught heck for it. I don't think she's hurt bad.

NANCY: They called us Huns.

MARTHA: If Mr. O'Rourke hadn't come —

O'ROURKE: Mr. Brubacher, I can guarantee ya young Jimmy won't do nothing like that agin. But I can't speak for some of the others.

ZEPP: Zank you.

O'ROURKE: You see, it makes some folks mad to see you all doing so well out of the war. Course you people always seem to do better than us, and now, we being short of hands —

ZEPP: If you haff need of help —

O'ROURKE: Might take you up on that, then. Paddy volunteered. Myself, I don't think much of the English. I remember what the bastards did in Ireland. You know, if you wouldn't mind a piece of advice — you might try not speaking that German so much in front of Canadians. Adds fuel to the fire. Well, goodnight.

ZEPP: Zank you.

MARTHA: Jah, thanks.

O'ROURKE: Oh, and Mrs. Brubacher, Bridget told me about the herb tea and that, and we really appreciate it, and you just come and talk to the Devil anytime you want. [*Exits.*]

HANNAH: What did he say?

LYDIE: Oh, I think he wants us to stop speaking German.

HANNAH: Jah, but after —

LYDIE: Put Nancy to bed, please, Martha. [*Girls exit.*]

HANNAH: No, well, my English isn't too good. About talking to —

LYDIE: When would you want her to start?

KATE: Oh, you mean it?

HANNAH: Could I have her Monday?

LYDIE: It's really up to Zepp.

HANNAH: Thank you both.

KATE: Martha, Martha, guess what! [*Runs off*]

ZEPP: I'll drive you home, Hannah.

HANNAH: Ach, no, I'll be sitting in my kitchen by the time you get hitched up. God bless you.

LYDIE: She's too young.

ZEPP: The Bible says, 'Be ye easily entreated.'

LYDIE: That tele-thing would have been handy, Zepp.

ZEPP: Enough.

LYDIE: We could have said no and stuck to it, if we didn't have to look her in the face.

[*Blackout*]

scene iii
Brubacher's and Bauman's
A few days later, after supper

LYDIE is washing the floor, the girls helping. ZEPP enters.

ZEPP: Would it be unhandy for you if I went away tomorrow?

LYDIE: With the oats still in the fields? I should say.

MARTHA: Oh, Mom, look where he's standing. [*Washing floor*]

ZEPP: I'm sorry, Martha.

LYDIE: I thought you were going threshing until it got dark?

ZEPP: Ah ... it's raining. If you didn't have to worry about the oats — [*Stepping on Martha's hand*]

MARTHA: Mom!

LYDIE: Zepp, sit down here. [*Sits him on a box*]

MARTHA: Where do you want to go, Doddy?

ZEPP: Oh —

LYDIE: Zepp Brubacher, there's not a cloud in the sky.

ZEPP: Jah, well.

LYDIE: Martha, we need clean water.

MARTHA: No, Mom, see.

LYDIE: I want two pails. Both of you go.

NANCY: Oh, Mom. [*They exit.*]

LYDIE: Lift your feet. Now, what is going on? [*She washes under the feet*]

ZEPP: The government men came out to the field. Said if I didn't have all the men registered by noon tomorrow, they'd put me in jail.

LYDIE: Ach, Zepp. They can't put all the men in jail.

ZEPP: They know.

LYDIE: Well, then. You can put your feet down now.

ZEPP: They said since I'm deacon, they start with me.

LYDIE: For how long?

ZEPP: Nine days.

LYDIE: That's not too bad.

ZEPP: Except, after that, if I don't register, there's another nine, and so on. [*Pause*]

LYDIE: I suppose the neighbours will do the threshing.

ZEPP: Jah, well.

LYDIE: Zepp?

ZEPP: There's a big fine for every day you don't sign, see. So the government may just take the farm, confiscate it or something. [*Silence*] Guess I might as well get back to it.

[*Moves to door*]

LYDIE: What for? [*Throws rag in pail*]

MARTHA: [ZEPP *crashes into her as she comes in*] Doddy!

ZEPP: Never mind, Martha. I think your mom's finished anyways. [*Exits*]

HANNAH: This batch is ready, Sarah.

KATE: I'm Kate, Hannah.

HANNAH: Oh, jah, you're you.

KATE: She was Mutti's best friend, wasn't she?

HANNAH: From the time they could walk. She was that glad when Lydie finally let Zepp marry her and they were neighbours again.

KATE: What happened to her?

HANNAH: She died when Yock was born.

KATE: I know, but why?

HANNAH: Ach, don't you be scared. She was always a delicate little thing. You'll have no trouble.

KATE: I hope not. I want lots of babies. All girls.

HANNAH: Ah, but Yock ... I mean, anyway, you have to take what you get. Sarah was set on giving Christy a son. He was like a madman when she died. We almost lost Yock, too. It was bitter cold. You'll never guess what I did.

KATE: What?

HANNAH: I bundled him up in the copper boiler and shoved it in the warmer.

YOCK: [*Enters*] Are you telling Katie how you did for me like I was a little piglet?

HANNAH: It worked.

KATE: Except you never changed.

YOCK: [*Stealing a cookie*] Ummm. You're not a bad cook.

KATE: Get out of there.

HANNAH: Where's the wax?

YOCK: Oh, I knew there was something else.

KATE: We don't have enough to finish.

HANNAH: Where do you keep your brains, boy?

YOCK: [*Taking wax from under his hat and out of pocket*] Right here?

HANNAH: He's that much like his father, Katie.

KATE: Yock is?

HANNAH: Oh, jah. I remember one time, we were having a quilting bee, for Sarah, it was, and these two strange women turned up. Well, we knew the Janzis were expecting company. It was half an hour before we found them out. [CHRISTY *enters*] It was Christy and Zepp dressed up.

YOCK: Did you really do that, Pa?

CHRISTY: There's mud all over the buggy.

YOCK: I was into town.

CHRISTY: Go wipe it off.

[YOCK *exits.*]

CHRISTY: How am I ever going to get respect from him with you telling him stories like that?

HANNAH: Would you put these in the pantry, Katie?

KATE: Sure, Hannah.

HANNAH: There's no harm in a little fun, Christy.

CHRISTY: I'm sorry. It's just he ...

[CHRISTY *takes his account book and begins making entries.*]

HANNAH: What?

CHRISTY: Everytime he finds a new way of spiting me.

HANNAH: Did you check on that farm?

CHRISTY: Do you really think a farm will make a difference?

HANNAH: Not by itself ... but ... [*Gesturing to where* KATE *has exited*] They're getting along well.

CHRISTY: What does that mean?

HANNAH: Ach, you men are slow sometimes.

CHRISTY: Katie?

HANNAH: Don't say a word.

[CHRISTY *is delighted.*]

HANNAH: Did you talk to Zepp?

CHRISTY: About Katie?

HANNAH: About making our own bishop?

CHRISTY: Oh, jah. Some folks would rather we share Jake Bender with East Zorra.

[KATE *re-enters.* CHRISTY *beams at her.*]

HANNAH: We won't be linked with the rubber church.

KATE: The what?

CHRISTY: You're too young to remember. That's what we used to call East Zorra when they let in rubber tires.

HANNAH: When my man first saw a buggy with them things for wheels, he said, 'Here comes the Devil, and now he's wearing bedroom slippers.'

[ALL *laugh.* CHRISTY *reaches for a cookie.*]

KATE: Christy, there'll be none left.

CHRISTY: Aw, just one more, Katie.

KATE: You're as bad as Yock. [*She takes cookies away*]

[CHRISTY *nods approval to* HANNAH.]

CHRISTY: You're a hard woman, like your mutti.

[YOCK *enters and washes at the washstand.* KATE *and* HANNAH *work Upstage.*]

CHRISTY: Yock? I was looking at that farm Isaac Stutzman's got for sale.

YOCK: What for?

CHRISTY: If you're interested, I might consider buying it.

HANNAH: You never know when a second farm might come in handy.

CHRISTY: The barn's falling down, but the land's been looked after. It's value.

YOCK: Don't you think we have enough?

CHRISTY: You could use something to keep you busy, maybe.

YOCK: It won't keep me from thinking for myself. [*Pause*]

CHRISTY: I didn't mean that.

YOCK: Pa, I went to Menno's meeting yesterday.

CHRISTY: His father told me. Why didn't you ask me?

YOCK: If I had, would you have let me go?

CHRISTY: I would not.

YOCK: What's wrong with some of us talking things out?

HANNAH: Young folks knowing better than their elders.

YOCK: The world is changing, pa.

CHRISTY: The world always changes, being a Christian doesn't.

HANNAH: That's why we stay separate.

YOCK: But we can't anymore. This is the biggest war in history.

CHRISTY: You didn't talk about the war? [*Genuinely shocked*]

YOCK: Pa, when our forefathers were talking about not fighting, wars then were just border skirmishes.

HANNAH: Big words.

YOCK: Now it's all kinds of countries.

CHRISTY: 'Nations are just a drop in the bucket and counted in the small dust of the balance.'

YOCK: What's that supposed to mean?

HANNAH: Heaven and hell are the only countries a Christian has to worry about.

CHRISTY: [*Trying*] Yock, our people stand for peace.

YOCK: Jah, but if we win this war, there'll be peace forever.

CHRISTY: Who is 'we'?

YOCK: Canada, the Empire.

CHRISTY: I let you stay in school too long.

YOCK: I'm sick of you always blaming school.

CHRISTY: And I'm sick of you quoting your learning at me. Listen to me, you don't get peace by fighting. If they tell you that, they're wrong. The high people have always had wars. They always will. We have peace here ... among ourselves. We obey God. We don't kill people. We don't take what's not ours. If the high people wanted peace, they'd do the same.

YOCK: It's not that simple, Pa.

CHRISTY: It is that simple. If everybody stayed home and minded their own business ...

YOCK: And made money!

CHRISTY: What?

YOCK: You don't seem to mind getting rich from the war, do you?

[*Silence.* CHRISTY, *faced with the choice of hitting* YOCK *or leaving the room, exits into the house.* YOCK *exits outside.*]

HANNAH: [*To* KATE] What makes a boy like that, do you know?

KATE: I don't understand most of it.

HANNAH: I'm going to bed.

KATE: I'll just stay up for a bit, chop some of these beans for tomorrow.

[KATE *lights an oil lamp.* HANNAH *exits.* KATE *sits down with pan and beans.* CHRISTY *comes back, picks up his account book and puts it away.*]

CHRISTY: Katie?

KATE: Jah, Christy?

CHRISTY: Yock is my son. [*This is difficult for him to say*] But you'd be careful, wouldn't you, with any young man?

KATE: You don't need to say that to me, Christy.

CHRISTY: I know, but —

KATE: And not to Yock either.

CHRISTY: Goodnight, then. [*Exits*]

[*In the Brubacher kitchen,* ZEPP *in night clothes is packing a small, old bag. He has an oil lamp.*]

LYDIE: [*Off*] Zepp, aren't you coming to bed?

ZEPP: Jah.

LYDIE: I've been waiting ten minutes.

ZEPP: Go to sleep if you want.

LYDIE: No. With you going away for who knows how long?
No! [*Enters*] What are you doing now?

ZEPP: I just thought of a few more things I might need.

[ZEPP *places a box of dominoes in his suitcase.*]

LYDIE: Oh, Zepp. Dominoes?

ZEPP: I might get a cell mate.

LYDIE: I was thinking ... if they're putting you in jail just because
you're deacon ...

ZEPP: Jah ...

LYDIE: Well, if Christy wants to be bishop ... [*As if to underline her
argument she unpacks the box of dominoes.*]

ZEPP: [*Underlining his response, he takes the dominoes from her and
repacks them.*] We can't make him bishop by tomorrow.

LYDIE: [*Takes dominoes out again*] He might be willing to start
ahead.

ZEPP: Be hard to explain to the government.

LYDIE: He'd enjoy going to jail more than you. And he don't
have a wife and young children.

ZEPP: You could manage better than Hannah.

LYDIE: [*Repacks the dominoes, acknowledging that she has lost the argument.*] I'm going to be awful lonely, Zepp.

ZEPP: Kate will only be a few days longer.

LYDIE: It's not Kate I'm going to be lonely for.

ZEPP: The Lord asks some hard things sometimes.

LYDIE: Come on to bed.

ZEPP: Just one minute. Fetch me my Bible. [LYDIE *passes him a
small Bible. As he starts to pack it, a letter falls out.*] What's
that?

LYDIE: That's that thing Sam Moyer brought to the door.

ZEPP: Who's Sam Moyer?

LYDIE: Some Mennonite from Vineland. Now that's where a tele-thing would have come in handy.

ZEPP: When? [*Reading letter*]

LYDIE: I guess it was when you were choring. Sure would have saved him a lot of travelling. Of course he was visiting in St. Jacobs.

ZEPP: You forgot to give it to me.

LYDIE: That's why I put it in the Bible, so I wouldn't forget.

ZEPP: Then you go and read the Martyr's Mirror, instead.

LYDIE: I thought it'd cheer us up about you going to jail. Where are you going, Zepp? Zepp! [ZEPP *puts on coat and hat over nightshirt and exits*]

[KATE *is still chopping vegetables.* YOCK *enters.*]

YOCK: I was hoping it would be you still up.

KATE: Oh, why?

YOCK: No reason.

KATE: Oh.

YOCK: Except maybe we could pretend that we'd been to a singing or something, and I'd just brought you home.

KATE: To your house?

YOCK: To your parlour. You'd make me some cocoa.

KATE: I could. [*She rises*]

YOCK: And we'd finished it already, and we sat down and turned down the lamps.

KATE: Not while I'm working here, folks'll talk.

YOCK: Do you care what folks say, Kate?

KATE: I don't want to give them reason to ... It's only for a little bit, then I'll be home.

YOCK: But we may not even like each other by then.

KATE: We won't have missed much, if we don't.

YOCK: On the other hand [*Takes her hand*] ... 'Thy lips are like a thread of scarlet, Honey and milk are under thy tongue.'

KATE: Yock, don't talk like that!

YOCK: Why not? It's in the Bible.

KATE: It is not!

YOCK: From the Song of Solomon. Here, I tore it out to memorize it. [*Shows page*]

KATE: Oh, Yock!

YOCK: You sound just like Grosmutti. You look like her, too. You really think wearing that thing on your head is going to get you into heaven?

KATE: Jacob Bauman!

YOCK: I bet you'd be pretty if you didn't wear those funny clothes.

KATE: Oh, like Moira O'Rourke?

YOCK: Jah, well, maybe. She's got that gorgeous hair.

KATE: That so?

YOCK: Real thick, with lots of colours in it.

KATE: Mine's just as good.

YOCK: Oh, I suppose there's nothing wrong with thin hair.

KATE: It's just the way it's pulled back so tight.

YOCK: Sure.

KATE: Look, smarty. [*Takes out a strand of hair*]

YOCK: Let me feel. Sure is soft. [*He pushes back her covering*] You're right. You're beautiful, Katie Brubacher. [KATE *pulls away*] No, don't go away.

KATE: You can come and visit me when I'm back home.

YOCK: Sit here awhile.

Kate Trotter (Kate) and Keith Thomas (Yock).

KATE: No, Yock, can't you wait?

YOCK: Promise you won't date anyone else.

KATE: [*With a show of reluctance*] Oh, all right.

YOCK: We're courting then?

KATE: [*About to agree*] Oh, but we can't!

YOCK: 'Cause I'm not baptised? I love you. I want to be with you. What the hell does that have to do with being baptised?

KATE: Your Pa'd wash your mouth out with soap if he heard you talk like that.

YOCK: If I take baptism class next year ... if I join ...

KATE: Well ...

YOCK: And Pa buys the Stutzman farm ...

KATE: It's a real nice place, Yock.

[*Knock at door.*]

YOCK: [*Peeking out*] It's your Pa!

KATE: [*She scurries to the door into the house*] Don't say anything, not yet. [*She exits*]

YOCK: [*Opening the door*] Zepp!

ZEPP: Your doddy in?

YOCK: [*Looking at the nightshirt under his coat*] What's the matter?

ZEPP: Nothing. I just dropped over for a cup of coffee.

CHRISTY: [*Coming in, also in nightshirt, and laughing at ZEPP*] Coffee, is it? [*To YOCK*] Time you were in bed.

YOCK: Jah, goodnight. [*Picks up paper with quote from table and exits*]

ZEPP: We can sign the cards.

CHRISTY: No!

ZEPP: I'm taking them 'round and getting them signed tonight.

CHRISTY: Too proud to go to jail, are you?

ZEPP: I don't mind going if I have to, but if you want a martyr...

CHRISTY: You're just getting old, old and soft.

ZEPP: You're getting old and stubborn. Now all we do is [*Takes letter from his pocket*] write Mennonite ... oh ... well, Amish — Mennonite, he means, across the top.

CHRISTY: What have you got there?

ZEPP: I wrote to Bishop Coffman.

CHRISTY: We make up our own minds here.

ZEPP: Now, if I go north as far as Zehr's and you go south to Martin's ...

CHRISTY: Me?

ZEPP: I've only got till noon tomorrow and I won't have to argue so much if you're doing it, too.

CHRISTY: The government will have our names. They'll come and put us in the army.

ZEPP: No, Bishop Coffman's been up to Ottawa. He's got it all worked out with Mr. Borden.

CHRISTY: Has he got it all worked out with God?

ZEPP: [*Reading from the letter*] 'And if any man doubt that registering with the nation is within the law of God, let him read Matthew 5, 41-45.'

CHRISTY: [*Thinks through the quote*] What about Matthew 5, 11 and 12?

ZEPP: [*Thinks it through*] 1 Peter 2, 13 and 14.

CHRISTY: Second Corinthians 10, 4.

ZEPP: Luke 2.

[*Pause.* CHRISTY *is stumped.*]

ZEPP: Your Bible handy?

[CHRISTY *finds his Bible and looks for the page.*]

ZEPP: [*Reeling it off from memory*] 'Then Augustus Caesar declared that every man should return to the place of his birth to be counted and that he should take with him ...'

CHRISTY: But were the Romans at war?

ZEPP: The Romans were always at war! Get your hat!

CHRISTY: I suppose you are the deacon. [*Puts on hat and coat over nightshirt*]

ZEPP: And we ain't got a bishop — yet.

CHRISTY: [*At door*] This is on your head.

ZEPP: [*As they exit*] And Luke's.

[*Blackout*]

scene iv
Special Recruitment Court in Kitchener
A week or so later

MENNO, YOCK, ZEPP and CHRISTY standing outside, ill at ease.

ZEPP: At least we get a day off work.

MENNO: If they let me go back to the farm, tomorrow I'll kiss the pigs.

CHRISTY: You can thank the deacon if you don't.

[MILITARY OFFICER *calls from inside.*]

OFFICER: Menno Miller.

MENNO: Jah? [ALL *enter*]

OFFICER: Why are you here?

MENNO: I got this in the mail.

OFFICER: This is your notice of conscription.

MENNO: My religion won't let me fight.

OFFICER: You may claim exemption if you are a conscientious objector to combatant service, and if you belong to a sect recognized as such by the Order in Council of 1873. [*Pause*] What is your sect? Your religion?

MENNO: Amish.

OFFICER: I can assign you to a noncombatant service such as the restricted medical corps. You would not have to carry a gun.

MENNO: Would I haf to wear a uniform?

OFFICER: The medical corps is part of the army.

MENNO: A Christian can't have anything to do with the army.

OFFICER: Ours is a Christian army.

MENNO: There's no such thing.

OFFICER: Place your hand on the Bible and swear that you —

MENNO: Excuse me, we never tell lies.

ZEPP: We don't believe in swearing. I have here ...

OFFICER: Who is that fellow?

ZEPP: Joseph Brubacher. Deacon of his church. It says here that we can affirm in the presence of witnesses.

[ZEPP *passes a letter to the* OFFICER. *The letter should look as if it has been in his pocket while he did the barn chores. A piece of straw might fall out.*]

OFFICER: You will affirm that Menno Miller was a member in good standing as of July 7, 1917.

ZEPP: Jah.

OFFICER: Say, 'I will.'

ZEPP: Jah, yes, I will.

OFFICER: [*Stamps letter and returns*] Jacob Bauman. And can these persons affirm that you are a member in good standing in the Amish sect?

ZEPP: Yes.

YOCK: No. I'm not a member of the church.

CHRISTY: Yock.

YOCK: I'm not baptised.

OFFICER: Report for induction by the tenth of this month.

ZEPP: No.

OFFICER: This hearing is over.

ZEPP: He will not fight.

OFFICER: Then he can spend the rest of the war in military prison.

ZEPP: He is Amish like the other. Born Amish, among Amish, you cannot say he is not. Other courts have not made this trouble.

OFFICER: You may appeal my decision to the provincial tribunal in Toronto.

ZEPP: But why, we lose our work? They will let him go.

OFFICER: They may, but I will not. [*Pause*] I have no use for pampering immigrants who came to this country with nothing, who prospered under the freedom granted to them by the Crown, and who now in the time of their country's need refuse to accept the responsibilities of citizenship. If it were not for politicians, you would be imprisoned for treason. Personally, I would like to see you shot.

CHRISTY: [*With difficulty*] We came with nossing. Jah. And there was nossing when we came. It was mine people built Ebytown or Berlin or Kitchener or whatever you choose to name it. We cleared all this part of this country. And never have we asked from anyone except you leave us alone. Before one Amish put a foot in Canada, my forefathers own went before your King George — he was German, too — in England and he gaf his own promise. No one Amish would have to fight ever. It is not the Amish who change. You speak of shooting, of putting in jail. All this we haf before. Our faith is of 400 years. You think we are as kindling that you break us across your knee?

OFFICER: I imagine your eloquence will be impressive in Toronto.

[CHRISTY *and* OTHERS *go out.*]

CHRISTY: Just what did you think you were doing?

YOCK: You told me not to lie, Pa.

ZEPP: We get to see Toronto next.

YOCK: Listen, what about the Medical Corps? Why can't I ...

CHRISTY: You don't open your mouth.

YOCK: Pa ...

CHRISTY: I'm telling you.

[YOCK *exits.*]

ZEPP: All the same, I've got to hand it to you, Christy. I never would have thought of saying all that.

[CHRISTY *and* ZEPP *look at each other.*]

[*Blackout*]

scene v
The exterior of the Baumans'
Late fall, afternoon.

A table for food is set Upstage.

MENNO and YOCK are bringing on baskets of field corn and arranging them in piles for shucking. If they use a wheelbarrow, it could be used to throw the husks in later.

YOCK: The buildings were five times as high as the barn. No, maybe more. And the people ... all going by so fast.

MENNO: But they let you go all right?

YOCK: Oh, jah. Pa knew the law better than the tribunal. He must have studied up. He'd practised his English, too. [*They laugh*] I saw trolleys carrying 50 or 60 people, no horses pulling them, either.

MENNO: [*Interested*] Jah?

YOCK: I saw what the twentieth century is going to be. I sure wish I could be a part of it.

MENNO: I don't see why we can't be. Look at this.

[MENNO *gives* YOCK *a leaflet.*]

YOCK: [*Reading*] 'The Ministry of Agriculture is desirous of placing a farm tractor on your land ...?'

MENNO: [*Excited*] Yock, they're willing to give you the machine, all we'd have to pay for is the gas ... think of the time we'd save ... time to preach the gospel.

YOCK: Jah ... but Pa ... and the elders ...

MENNO: We been talking about it at Sunday school ... You should come again and tell us about the people in the city ... They're all heathens, aren't they?

KATE: [*Coming out with a tray of food*] You talking or working?

YOCK: I was just telling Menno about —

KATE: [*Joining in*] About the twentieth century. [*To* MENNO] I'm surprised he came back.

YOCK: [*Crossing to help her*] Pa never let go of my collar the whole time. [*Whispers*] Besides, I had to come back for you.

[KATE *smiles and exits back to house.*]

MENNO: You sure are lucky having her. Mom hired that Barbara Weber.

[YOCK *grins.*]

YOCK: That why you're hanging around here so much?

[ZEPP *enters.*]

YOCK: Lydie not coming?

ZEPP: Right behind me. [*Takes* YOCK's *arm*] Dan Yoder had a word with me.

YOCK: Oh. We weren't really dancing, Zepp.

ZEPP: No?

YOCK: More like just stomping our feet.

ZEPP: Hmmmm.

YOCK: Are you going to tell Pa?

ZEPP: Depends.

YOCK: On what?

ZEPP: On your handing over whatever it was you were just stomping your feet to?

[YOCK *sheepishly takes a mouth organ from his pocket.* ZEPP *slips it into his.*]

ZEPP: Yock, your doddy is bishop now and that means ...

[ZEPP *breaks off as* CHRISTY *comes out with wine jug for the table.*]

CHRISTY: [*Seeing* ZEPP *and* YOCK] What's going on there?

ZEPP: Oh, nothing. [*He joins* CHRISTY]

[HANNAH *and* KATE *come out as* LYDIE *and the* GIRLS *enter, followed by the* MILLERS. HANNAH *can greet* ESTHER.]

CHRISTY: [*To* LYDIE] About time you got here.

LYDIE: Ach, I was hoping you'd be done by now. [*Hugs* KATE] Why, Katie, girl, did you do all this? [*Refers to food*]

CHRISTY: She wouldn't be your daughter if she wasn't a good worker.

HANNAH: [*To* NANCY] Will you partner me, Nancy?

NANCY: Sure, Hannah.

[*The* GROUP *forms couples and begins to shuck. Young people are shy.* KATE *and* MARTHA *choose piles and wait.*]

MENNO: [*To* KATE] You need a hand, Katie?

YOCK: [*Rushing over*] She's taken already, [*Sotto*] for good.

KATE: Martha needs a partner, Menno.

[*While* KATE *is turned away,* YOCK *slips a red ear into her corn.*]

MARTHA: Oh, Katie.

MENNO: [*Without a lot of grace*] Jah, all right.

[*Husking starts. Someone begins a song softly. People join in.*]

CHRISTY: I can clear this pile faster than both of you.

ZEPP: Ach, your mouth works faster than your hands.

[CHRISTY *and* ZEPP *shuck furiously, urged on by others. Singing swells.*]

MARTHA: We saw it. [KATE *has red ear of corn*]

LYDIE: Is it red?

ZEPP: Jah, it is.

KATE: No, it's just the sunset on it.

CHRISTY: Give it here. Mutti?

HANNAH: Jah, it's red. [*Everyone comes over to them*]

YOCK: Aw, do I have to? I'm afraid of spoiling my appetite.

KATE: You pig. [*He kisses her quickly on the cheek*]

[*Laughter.*]

LYDIE: Remember the time Sarah brained you with the cob, Christy? Because someone told her you put it in the stack yourself?

ZEPP: Now, who would have told her a thing like that?

CHRISTY: 'As water spilled on the ground that cannot be gathered up again'!

ZEPP: It all comes from God. I want you all to know, now that Christy's bishop, you better not get caught dancing in his washhouse.

HANNAH: The girls are going to have to dress decent, too.

CHRISTY: All the same, [*To* ZEPP] I want an absolute stop put to that kind of thing. You're going to have to be a bit more serious about being deacon.

ZEPP: I don't suppose you remember a barn raising years ago when my brother Pete got married.

CHRISTY: I do not.

ZEPP: You don't remember being a fair hand with one of these [*Pulls out mouth organ*]

CHRISTY: I suppose you took that off my son.

ZEPP: You don't remember begging old Deacon Zehr not to tell your doddy? [*Puts it to mouth*]

CHRISTY: I do recall that letting you play drove all the boys back to the kitchen. [*Grabs it, puts it to his lips, then throws it away*] Thought you had me, didn't you, Deacon Brubacher?

ZEPP: I just think we're too soon old and —

CHRISTY: Too old, smart.

[*Singing heard in distance.*]

O'ROURKE: 'Where are the legs with which you run
When first you went to carry a gun

Susie Walsh (Nancy), Deanna Bearrs (child), Rachel Thompson (child), Sam Robinson (Zepp), Janet Amos (Lydie), Kate Trotter (Kate), Denise Kennedy (Martha), Keith Thomas (Yock) and Beth Amos (Hannah).

For sure your dancing days are done.'

[O'ROURKE *lurches on. Women gather children and rush them as far out of his way as possible.*]

O'ROURKE: Bring on the Huns.

YOCK: Mr. O'Rourke.

O'ROURKE: All you God-fearing Christians will have to forgive me. I'm celebrating. My boy's coming home.

YOCK: I'm glad, sir.

O'ROURKE: All you Huns are glad. He was a terror to you.

HANNAH: What's he saying?

YOCK: Paddy is coming home.

O'ROURKE: Don't you dare to speak his name in that filthy tongue.

CHRISTY: We are happy for you, but we would prefer not here.

O'ROURKE: 'Course not all of him is coming.

YOCK: What do you mean?

O'ROURKE: What do you care? You still got your legs, you stinking little yellow bastard. Don't you know what you did to my Pat?

[O'ROURKE *shoves or physically threatens* YOCK.]

CHRISTY: This has nossing to do with us.

O'ROURKE: We're going to run you out of this country. The boys won't be sharing it with the likes of you, that keep your sons safe and see ours ruined.

CHRISTY: Go now. We will pray for the son.

[O'ROURKE *spits on* CHRISTY.]

O'ROURKE: The Virgin herself would damn your prayers to hell.
[*Exits*]
[*Off*] 'Sure you'll have to be put with bowl to beg
Paddy, I hardly knew ya.'

CHRISTY: There's nothing to worry about. Let's all go back to work.

YOCK: No wonder they hate us.

CHRISTY: Yock.

YOCK: He was my friend, Pa.

CHRISTY: 'Those who live by the sword' –

YOCK: Jah, die by it. Except they're dying for us so we can stay here and sing these stupid hymns. [*Kicks basket of corn.*]

CHRISTY: Control yourself.

YOCK: Pa, I just want to know. What makes us so special? Tell me that.

CHRISTY: You know the answer.

YOCK: Did God stop with the Amish? Is nobody Christian but us?

CHRISTY: No Christian resists evil. No Christian kills.

YOCK: What do you think Paddy is? Pa, if it weren't for boys like him, the Germans would have walked right in and taken over by now.

CHRISTY: Let them.

YOCK: Let them? You know what they'd do to Kate, to Grosmutti even? They'd line the children up against the wall and shoot them. Are you so sure you'd be against fighting then?

CHRISTY: I have never asked Paddy O'Rourke or anyone else to go and get shot trying to protect me or mine. Christ died for us, that was enough.

YOCK: Did He? Well, I never asked Him to. [*Pause*]

[CHRISTY *is genuinely shocked and outraged.*[

CHRISTY: Get into that woodshed. Get. [*He forces* YOCK *off. Silence.*]

KATE: He didn't mean it. He knew Paddy at school. He can't help ... [*Starting to follow them*]

LYDIE: Katie, don't. Come over here.

KATE: He didn't mean that about the Lord, Mutti. I know he didn't.

LYDIE: I should hope not. But Kate, people can't go around saying things like that, even if they don't mean them.

[*The sounds of a severe beating are heard.*]

ZEPP: Jah, but this is between father and son. We just keep on with our work. [*Silence*]

LYDIE: Well, let's serve all that food you and Hannah made. Could we do that now, Hannah?

HANNAH: You go ahead, Lydie. I'm not hungry. [*Exits into house*]

LYDIE: Oh, well. Zepp?

[CHRISTY *strides back and into the house without looking at anyone. All pretense of being able to continue fails.*]

ZEPP: I guess we're about done anyways.

LEVI: [*Stopping* MENNO *from following* CHRISTY] Menno!

[*The* MILLERS *exit silently.*]

LYDIE: Katie, do you want to come home with us, now? I think she should, Zepp.

[KATE, *alone, keeps shucking.*]

ZEPP: And leave Hannah to clear all this up?

LYDIE: All right, but you be careful, Katie.

[ALL *exit.* KATE *continues working. After a moment* YOCK *comes in and stands apart from her. He has been physically hurt as well as humiliated.*]

KATE: Yock, are you ...

YOCK: Leave me alone.

KATE: Please.

YOCK: Oh, Katie.

KATE: Did he hurt you bad?

YOCK: I've got to get away from him.

KATE: You're just feeling shamed.

YOCK: Don't tell me how I'm feeling. [*Pause*] Katie, would you come away with me, right now?

KATE: Where?

YOCK: Anywhere ... away from here.

KATE: You want me to go where I know nobody and nobody knows me?

YOCK: Listen, Katie ... if I stay here I might as well be dead. I can find work ... maybe it'll be hard for awhile, but at least I'll know I'm alive.

KATE: When you're burning in hell, it'll be a great comfort.

YOCK: If God's like Pa says He is, I don't care if I burn.

KATE: That's blasphemy! [*She turns to go in, but comes back*] I can't run out on my folks, Yock.

YOCK: Not even for me?

KATE: I can't live without love.

YOCK: I love you.

KATE: I mean the church, and our own people.

YOCK: I never felt that love. I keep hearing about it. But I never felt it. [*Pause*] You won't come? [*Pause*] I knew you wouldn't.

KATE: When we take the Stutzman farm, we'll be away from your pa. [*Silence*] Come in to the house, please.

YOCK: You go in.

KATE: Not without you.

[YOCK *puts his hands on her shoulders.*]

YOCK: I'm all right, Katie, don't worry. I just want to be alone for a bit.

KATE: But ... you won't ...

YOCK: I said, 'Go in.' Goodnight.

[KATE *exits reluctantly.* YOCK *stands for a moment.*]

[*Fade out*]

END OF ACT ONE

David Fox (Christy).

Act II, scene i
Brubacher's kitchen and the exterior of Bauman's kitchen
Early summer, 1918
Suppertime

In the Brubacher kitchen, KATE is sitting at the table, staring into space.

The sound of hammering or tinkering comes from outside the Bauman house.

HANNAH is inside setting the table.

HANNAH: [*Calling out*] Aren't you coming in to your supper?

CHRISTY: [*Outside*] Not while there's light enough for fixing.

HANNAH: Lena Schultz told me her Levi's looking for a place to work.

CHRISTY: I won't hire another man's son.

HANNAH: I been going over it and over it. I don't know where we went wrong.

[LYDIE *and* MARTHA *enter Brubacher's kitchen with baskets of strawberries.*]

LYDIE: Kate! The table's not even laid.

KATE: It's early.

LYDIE: Your doddy is not two steps behind me.

KATE: I just sat down for a minute.

LYDIE: In the middle of the day! You're not sick, are you?

MARTHA: She's moping over you know who!

LYDIE: Ach, she's got more sense than that.

[LYDIE, MARTHA *and* KATE *set table and prepare food.*]

[HANNAH *ladles soup, cuts bread, etc.*]

HANNAH: As soon as he could walk, he took off down that lane. I used to have to tie him onto the porch rail if I wanted to

get any work done. I remember one time, he offered
Mose Yoder a penny to cut him loose. Mose wouldn't, of
course, so he offered him two pennies to buy his pocket
knife. And him only this high. The Lord will keep him
safe and bring him home again. Then there'll be more joy
in heaven than over the 99. In the meantime, [*Calling out to*
CHRISTY] your soup's getting cold.

[ZEPP *and* MENNO *enter the Brubacher side of the stage.*]

MENNO: I can spare an hour tonight. I have a study group later on.

ZEPP: You're getting together at night, too, are you?

MENNO: Jah. I mean, we don't need permission just to talk, do we?

ZEPP: Well ...

[ZEPP *and* MENNO *enter the kitchen.*]

ZEPP: [*To* LYDIE] Menno's staying.

MENNO: If it's not unhandy.

MARTHA: Oh, we've lots.

LYDIE: Where's Nancy?

KATE: Doing her homework.

LYDIE: [*Calling*] Nancy! [To OTHERS] That girl, I can't keep her
away from a book.

ZEPP: Ach, what's the harm?

[CHRISTY *enters* HANNAH'*s kitchen and washes.*]

LYDIE: Knowledge puffs up. You don't want her to turn out like
... some.

[NANCY *enters from inside the house.*]

ZEPP: Not chicken stew again.

LYDIE: There's no sense feeding them anymore, and they're too
tough to fry.

NANCY: [*Chanting*] 'Use them up, wear them out.
Make them do, or do without.'

ZEPP: Make them stew or do without.

[*The* BRUBACHER'S *sit.*]

MENNO: Mom's keeping hers. She figures the store will start buying eggs from us again as soon as the war's over.

[CHRISTY *and* HANNAH *sit and bow their heads in a silent Grace.*]

ZEPP: When's that going to be?

MENNO: They say by July for certain.

LYDIE: I tried to give a couple of dozen to Mrs. O'Rourke the other day, and she just pelted them at me. It's lucky the high people can't ...

[ZEPP *bows his head for Grace.* ALL *bow their heads for a moment.*]

LYDIE: [*As heads come up*] ... aim.

ZEPP: Now reach and help yourselves.

[*Plates are passed.* MENNO *is shy, and his is empty when others start eating.*]

ZEPP: I think we have too many girls for him.

LYDIE: I think we've got too many for us. Kate should hire out again.

KATE: Oh, Mutti, I worked out all winter.

LYDIE: You can't sit around here dreaming.

ZEPP: Dreaming?

MENNO: Becky Zimmerman told Mum Kate was the best worker she ever had.

KATE: I just want to stay home for awhile.

LYDIE: Will you promise to get some work into your hands anytime you start thinking about what you shouldn't be thinking about?

KATE: I do. I try.

LYDIE: Then we'll see. What about you, Menno? You going to be hiring out all the time?

MENNO: 'Till I have a bit of cash put together, anyway.

LYDIE: Now what would a young bachelor want with cash? Planning something?

MENNO: Oh, no, no. [*Blush, giggle*] I want a farm of my own, that's all.

ZEPP: I hope you don't think I can afford them kind of wages.

MENNO: Oh, no. Pa's buying the old Stutzman place for me.

[KATE *goes to the stove to cover her confusion.*]

MENNO: I need seed money, and [*taking breath*] Rube is thinking about buying one of them tractor outfits. I might go in with him.

ZEPP: Oh?

MENNO: I could sure get the farm going faster.

ZEPP: You'll get the bishop going faster, too.

MARTHA: Oh, that Christy Bauman makes me so mad. All he's doing is preaching about what we're doing wrong.

ZEPP: Martha.

MARTHA: Did you hear what he said last week about the young people being willful? He should talk.

ZEPP: Enough.

MENNO: But, you know, Zepp, there's nothing in the Bible about not using machines. There's nothing about not wearing a mustache, either.

ZEPP: You want a mustache now? [*Giggles from the* GIRLS]

LYDIE: What about 'Be ye separate'?

MENNO: We think that means in our hearts, in doing good. Like the war relief, or spreading the gospel.

ZEPP: Who's 'we'?

MENNO: The Bible class.

LYDIE: Menno?

MENNO: Jah, Lydie?

LYDIE: What does your Bible class think about telephones?

[ZEPP*'s look creates silence.*]

[CHRISTY *finishes his soup.*]

HANNAH: I was going to bake, but I felt that tired.

CHRISTY: Ach, there's no need of baking.

HANNAH: Dan's Mary was saying they were looking for a field to rent.

CHRISTY: Now, you're the one that's tired.

HANNAH: Son, you're not giving enough time to the church.

CHRISTY: I'm giving more than the members seem to want.

HANNAH: I'm not talking about preaching.

CHRISTY: Seems to me the more I preach against machines, the more my flock goes out and buys them.

HANNAH: You don't get stray sheep back by yelling at the ones that stayed put.

CHRISTY: Maybe the merchants should pay me. I could give up farming altogether.

HANNAH: You have to hike out and sit in kitchens and tell them right from wrong.

CHRISTY: Sometimes I think the church is going to be swallowed whole ...

HANNAH: Christy, listen to me, your doddy ...

CHRISTY: And there's nothing I can do about it.

HANNAH: Your doddy spent half his time visiting.

CHRISTY: I had to marry that Yoder girl to Rube Meyer last month. And her in the pink dress and him with his beard shaved off. And I stood there and said the holy words, because when it was on the tip of my tongue to send them home out of it, I looked in their eyes and all I could see was my son laughing at me.

HANNAH: That's got nothing to do with your duty.

CHRISTY: Do you think I would have been made bishop if Yock had run off before? Do you?

[CHRISTY *exits to outside.*]

[*The* BRUBACHERS *have finished eating.*]

LYDIE: Give the cloth a shake, will you, Katie?

MENNO: You need a hand?

[KATE *goes outside to shake a dishcloth. He follows.*]

MENNO: That was a good supper, Katie.

KATE: I hope you got enough to eat.

MENNO: Kate, I wanted to ask you something?

KATE: Jah?

MENNO: You never come to our Bible meetings?

KATE: I just never get 'round to it.

MENNO: All the crowd comes.

KATE: I think it's good, what you're doing. [*Laughs*] And you're sure learning to talk.

MENNO: Just about God's work ... I still get all mixed up ... when ... The meeting's at Yoder's tonight. Susan was saying she hasn't seen you since her wedding.

KATE: I'll see.

MENNO: I could give you a ride.

KATE: I said 'I'll see.' [*She turns to go in*]

MENNO: About Yock.

KATE: What?

MENNO: I had a letter.

KATE: From Yock?

MENNO: He wanted you to know he was all right.

KATE: Is he coming home?

MENNO: No. No, he's not.

KATE: Where is he?

MENNO: You're better off not knowing.

KATE: Menno, you've got to tell Christy at least.

MENNO: The bishop doesn't need me telling him about his son.

KATE: What does that mean?

MENNO: If it weren't for him ... Yock would never have ... Oh, never mind.

KATE: What are you talking about?

[ZEPP *comes out.*]

ZEPP: [*To* MENNO] I thought you'd be getting a head start.

MENNO: Well, I just ...

[KATE *goes into the house.*]

ZEPP: We better be at it. I want to finish under the new moon.

MENNO: That's just heathen superstition, you know.

ZEPP: I know when the corn goes higher.

[THEY *exit.*]

LYDIE: I can't believe the change in Menno. Maybe there is something up between him and Rachel Gingerich.

MARTHA: Oh, Mom, she's ancient.

LYDIE: Only a year older than Kate. Sure are lots getting married. Susan, and now Lizzie Martin is published. One thing for certain, when they all start having babies, there won't be any shortage of places to work out.

KATE: Mom, I think I'll take some of these over to Hannah. [*Picks up strawberries*] She was saying she was having a hard time bending over to pick. [*Exits*]

LYDIE: Can't you wait until ... [*Sees* KATE *is gone*]

MARTHA: Do you really think that's true, about Menno and Rachel?

LYDIE: It doesn't matter now, Martha ... She didn't hear a word we said. [*Seeing* MARTHA's *face*] Oh, dear, you're too young for him yet.

[ZEPP *and* MENNO *are seeding with a hand seeder and lanterns.*]

ZEPP: Looks like you can pick the stars out of the sky tonight, they're that close.

MENNO: I'd sure like to pick a bunch for the girls.

ZEPP: Funny how it all fits together, isn't it? There's you and me working out here. And you know God is going to make the shoots start up, when He gets 'round to it. [*Shows a handful of seeds*] And then the shock of corn will come up in its season.

MENNO: Zepp, are you trying to say something?

ZEPP: I guess I don't know how to explain it to a smart fellow like you.

MENNO: Now, don't get sneaky on me.

ZEPP: Menno, I don't think you can put machines out here and keep that business of fitting together. And something that's going to change that had better be pretty important.

MENNO: The word of God is important. That's what we ought to be planting. And not just in our own fields.

ZEPP: I suppose we got a choice ... we can talk about the word of God ... or we can live it. Now, I'm not sure which the Lord would prefer, but I'm sure He'll never be short of those wanting to talk.

[THEY *work their way off stage.*]

[CHRISTY *is sitting alone in the dark at his table. A small gadget is on the table, but he is lost in thought.* KATE *knocks at the door.* CHRISTY *lights an oil lamp hastily and picks up his work.* KATE *enters carrying berries.*]

CHRISTY: Kate, what brings you over?

KATE: Mom sent these for Hannah.

CHRISTY: She's upstairs. [KATE *doesn't move*] What is it?

KATE: Christy, do you know where Yock is?

CHRISTY: I don't want to hear his name.

KATE: You're all just pretending he doesn't exist.

CHRISTY: What's got into you, girl?

KATE: Yock wrote to Menno.

CHRISTY: What did he say? Kate? Answer me.

KATE: Menno wouldn't tell me. But he'd have to tell you if you asked him. [*No response*] Then I could go and bring him home.

CHRISTY: I don't want him home.

KATE: Your own son! No wonder he ran off.

CHRISTY: He ran off on you, too, and on Mutti.

KATE: But now, maybe he's lonely ... maybe he thinks we wouldn't be glad to see him ...

CHRISTY: You heard him that night.

KATE: He was just ...

CHRISTY: You heard him! He spit on you, on me, on the church, on Christ himself. [*Returning to his work, which he continues*] Don't waste your tears, Katie. He's been nothing but sorrow since the day he was born.

KATE: That's not true. You wouldn't listen to him. You just tried to break him, that's all you ever did.

CHRISTY: I did my duty. [*Speaking very directly to her*] Now, you listen. I'm talking as your bishop. You put that boy out of your mind. What are we put on earth for? Kate?

Kate Trotter (Kate) and David Fox (Christy).

KATE: To serve God.

CHRISTY: Your life isn't your own to waste feeling sorry for yourself. A good Christian woman is supposed to make a good Christian home, isn't that right? Get a good man, one who'll bring up your children the way the Lord would want. You want babies, don't you? Seems to me you and Mutti talked of nothing else.

KATE: Jah, but ...

CHRISTY: You'll forget about him in time.

KATE: I won't. Not about Yock.

CHRISTY: You're putting your will above doing your duty. That is not serving God, and you know it.

[*Silence.*]

CHRISTY: You're causing your parents pain and worry, too.

KATE: Has Mom been talking to you?

CHRISTY: I got eyes of my own. I know how they feel, seeing you get sadder every day, and not being able to do anything to help. I watched the life go out of you. I watch your mom and doddy worrying, and all because of my son. Get on with your life, Katie.

KATE: I try.

CHRISTY: Work, girl, keep going. Don't give yourself a moment to think. 'The days pass, swifter than a weaver's shuttle.' It does get easier. Kate, we're only promised happiness in heaven. All this is just a means of getting there. Keep your mind on God, and on the living. No matter how hard it is.

KATE: But he's not dead?

CHRISTY: As far as we're concerned, yes, he is. [*Pause*] Go on home, Katie, and do something nice for Mom. Don't talk about this to Mutti, will you? She shouldn't end her days without hope.

KATE: I won't.

CHRISTY: Thank your mom for the berries.

KATE: Jah. [*Exits*]

CHRISTY: [*After* KATE *is clear, softly*] God bless you.

HANNAH: Is that you? Is that you? [*Coming on*]

CHRISTY: It's just me, Mutti.

HANNAH: I thought I heard someone.

CHRISTY: Kate brought these over.

HANNAH: How kind of her. I'll make a pie.

CHRISTY: I like them just the way they are. [*Pours wine*]

HANNAH: Ach, I'm not so sick I can't make a bit of pastry. [*Picks up wine jug*]

CHRISTY: I'm not finished with that.

HANNAH: Your father never took more than a glass at a time.

CHRISTY: I'm not the man my father was. [HANNAH *puts jug away*]

[KATE *enters her kitchen, where* LYDIE *has left a lamp on low for her. She turns it up, picks up a Bible from the table, and opens it at random.*]

KATE: 'He shall return no more to his house. Neither shall his hearth know him anymore.' [*Closes Bible and starts to hull strawberries purposefully*]

[*Blackout*]

scene ii
The Brubacher kitchen and exterior
High summer, 1918

KATE and MENNO's wedding day.

The noise of celebrating is heard from off stage. Singing, clapping, laughter, etc.

HANNAH enters and sits wearily.

LYDIE: [*Coming in with a jug to be refilled ... or returning plates*] Hannah, what's wrong?

HANNAH: I just laughed too hard.

LYDIE: [*Looking closely at her*] Till the tears came?

HANNAH: Come on, you were going to show me the wedding gifts.

LYDIE: They're in her bedroom. [*Remembering*] Oh, it's not her bedroom anymore.

KATE: [*Entering*] What are you two doing here?

LYDIE: Why, it's Katie Miller.

KATE: I wonder if I'll ever get used to that.

HANNAH: Well, don't expect me to remember.

KATE: Hannah Miller, will you remember her?

HANNAH: Who's she?

KATE: My first baby girl.

CHRISTY: [*Entering*] Mutti, I was wondering where you were.

HANNAH: Just resting a minute.

CHRISTY: I'll take you home if you're tired.

ESTHER: [*Entering*] You going to show us the wedding gifts, Lydie?

LYDIE: Come on then.

ZEPP: [*Entering*] Where's Christy?

CHRISTY: Right here.

ZEPP: They're wanting another toast.

LYDIE: Wait till we come back. [*The* WOMEN *exit*]

CHRISTY: I am not toasting your daughter in lemonade.

ZEPP: Jah, well, Menno didn't want me to serve wine.

CHRISTY: What did you agree for?

ZEPP: Didn't seem worth fighting about.

CHRISTY: What I've got most against them Sunday schoolers is that they think they're holier than Jesus.

ZEPP: Jah, well.

CHRISTY: There's nothing to stop us from having a drop. [*Pours from jug*] I hope he took enough time off from studying to learn what to do tonight.

ZEPP: Well, I'm pretty sure it's in the Bible.

CHRISTY: You know, anytime I hear of trouble lately, I hear Menno's name at the bottom of it.

ZEPP: Like what?

CHRISTY: I drove past Meyer's last Sunday. I heard a lot of fancy singing – in English.

ZEPP: The High German is hard for the young folk ... they get English at school and ...

CHRISTY: That was the whole reason for allowing Sunday school in the first place.

ZEPP: You're right.

CHRISTY: Remember when we were so sure Menno wouldn't be able to give us much trouble?

ZEPP: The Lord sure gave him the words.

CHRISTY: I don't think it's the Lord. I'm hoping that Kate will straighten him out ... and his doddy-in-law, too. [*Pause*] You see, I want to leave this church the way my father left it ... That means I'm drawing up a list ... and there's not one more machine coming onto our fields ... and those that have them are going to have to give them up.

ZEPP: Now, you should put that to a meeting first.

CHRISTY: Well, you call one, Deacon, and the sooner the better.

[MENNO *enters with* LEVI. LEVI'*s eyes light up when he sees the jug.*]

MENNO: We were looking for Kate.

KATE: [*Entering*] We're right here.

ESTHER: [*The* WOMEN *follow* KATE] Oh, son, you'll never have to buy another pot for your kitchen.

LEVI: We're waiting for that toast.

CHRISTY: Jah, bring the jug, Zepp. [*To* MENNO] 'Wine maketh glad the heart of man,' Menno.

MENNO: I've got Katie for that.

CHRISTY: It's lucky your son wasn't at Cana, Levi. We'd still be waiting for the first miracle.

LEVI: That's right, Menno, you hear that.

[HANNAH *and* CHRISTY *go into house.*]

MENNO: Pa! Can't you leave the jug here, Zepp?

LEVI: Oh, Menno.

ZEPP: For the sake of peace?

MENNO: I didn't invite Susan and Rube for the sake of peace. I've kept this beard for the sake of peace.

LEVI: Son, hold your tongue for it now.

KATE: Menno, please.

MENNO: Oh, Katie, it's just that Christians shouldn't drink. You know that.

KATE: Are you saying that my doddy and Christy aren't Christians?

MENNO: You saw what happened at Susan and Rube's wedding.

KATE: I think there was something wrong with the wine.

MENNO: Funny it only bothered the bishop.

KATE: Menno, I don't know the Bible as well as you do, but I know that's not Christian.

MENNO: Jah, you're right. I'm going to need your good sense sometime.

KATE: Jah, you are.

MENNO: 'A good woman is a prize above rubies.' I'll find a way to make you happy.

KATE: I just want a home and babies and our way of life.

CHRISTY: [*Off*] I'm supposed to be toasting the young married couple. They seem a bit scarce.

[*A knock at the door.* KATE *opens it.*]

O'ROURKE: [*Entering*] I'm sorry to interrupt.

KATE: [*Calling off*] Mom.

LYDIE: [*Coming out*] Why, Mr. O'Rourke. I gif you velcome. Ve are making vedding, mine dochter for.

O'ROURKE: I figured. We heard the singing.

ZEPP: Ve make so much noise?

O'ROURKE: Oh, no, Paddy likes to listen to the music. Why I came over – Is Mr. Bauman here? I was wondering if he heard the news.

LYDIE: [*Calling*] Christy. Mr. O'Rourke wants to talk to you.

CHRISTY: [*Entering*] Jah?

O'ROURKE: Jimmy, my youngest, he was in town, picked up a paper. We was wondering if youse heard the news.

LYDIE: The war, it is all?

[*The* OTHERS *enter the kitchen.*]

O'ROURKE: It's not over, no, but nearly. September, they say, for certain. But it's about your son, Jake, he's a hero! Knocked out a whole German trench or something.

HANNAH: Yock, is he talking about Yock?

MARTHA: Wait, listen.

O'ROURKE: Yock, that's what you call him. He killed a whole bunch single-handed.

KATE: I don't believe it!

[MENNO *looks away.*]

HANNAH: What is he saying, what?

O'ROURKE: The Missus cut out the page. I brought it over. I thought you'd be happy. We're all some proud of him, I can tell you. Bet there'll be a grand parade when he gets home, eh?

HANNAH: [*Reading paper*] Jacob Bauman — what else? He is dead, is he dead?

MARTHA: No, no, he's ...

ZEPP: Hush.

HANNAH: Don't hush. Tell me, Christy.

O'ROURKE: What's the matter? Don't she understand?

LYDIE: She don't make out the English so good. Is nossing. We giff thanks you for coming, jah.

O'ROURKE: Aren't you going to tell her Yock [*Salutes and mimes shooting*] ... Guess nobody can call you people cowards now, eh? German lovers, neither.

LYDIE: [*Motioning him to door*] Jah.

O'ROURKE: Oh, and the Missus sent this along for the bride. Now this came all the way from Ireland [*linen tablecloth.*]

HANNAH: [*To* CHRISTY] What is this word?

CHRISTY: I'll tell you at home, Mutti.

MENNO: It's too fine for us.

LYDIE: Katie will make it best for.

O'ROURKE: Well, I'll be going, then. Don't want to interrupt the celebrating.

ZEPP: Jah, gutt, thanks.

O'ROURKE: If any of youse want to come over to our place for a drop of the hard stuff after – well, you'll be welcome as the flowers in May. [*Exits*]

[EVERYONE *talks at once.*]

ZEPP: Enough.

HANNAH: A soldier, that's what it is. Yock ...

LYDIE: Hannah, sit down.

HANNAH: No, I'm all right.

KATE: Hannah ...

HANNAH: I'm not letting anything spoil your day. Come on, Martha, Nancy, let's sing our song for your sister. Menno, take your bride to her corner.

CHRISTY: It's as we said, Katie. Don't stop smiling.

MARTHA: [*Taking* KATE's *hand*] Kate, I'm glad you have Menno to look after you now.

CHRISTY: Everyone back to the parlour.

LYDIE: Are you sure?

CHRISTY: [*Gesturing to the others*] Jah, come. Go.

[ZEPP *and* CHRISTY *remain in the kitchen. Silence.*]

ZEPP: You don't have to bear this alone, you know.

[CHRISTY *stands silent. Singing begins offstage. As soon as it is well underway,* HANNAH *returns.*]

HANNAH: [*To* CHRISTY] I need my rest now, son. [CHRISTY *helps her with shawl and bonnet*] [*To* ZEPP] Goodnight, Zepp. Katie is a lovely bride.

ZEPP: God keep you both.

[CHRISTY *and* HANNAH *exit. Once outside,* HANNAH *stumbles.*]

CHRISTY: Mutti!

HANNAH: Hush, it's just a spell.

CHRISTY: Let me call Lydie.

HANNAH: No, we've saddened them enough.

CHRISTY: Stay here then, I'll get the buggy.

HANNAH: Just let me stop a bit. [*Pause*] I never thought I'd be afraid to go home.

CHRISTY: What?

HANNAH: To heaven, I mean.

CHRISTY: Mutti, why?

HANNAH: How can I face your Sarah? How can I tell her the baby she handed me on her death bed is going to be burning in hell?

[*Blackout*]

scene iii
Brubacher kitchen, Bauman kitchen
Winter, 1918
Early evening

ZEPP is pacing, LYDIE sewing.

CHRISTY's house is messy and cheerless. CHRISTY is sitting with his jug.

LYDIE: Oh, Zepp, you're wearing a path in the floor.

ZEPP: Jah. [*Sits and immediately starts pacing again*]

LYDIE: Zepp!

ZEPP: [*Going by the window*] I was just wondering if it started snowing again.

[*Knock at door.* MENNO *and* KATE *enter. Both are nervous,* KATE *agitated.*]

LYDIE: Katie, girl.

KATE: I thought since Menno was driving over, I'd come visit.

ZEPP: You want a cup of coffee before we go, Menno?

MENNO: I'd rather just get it over with.

ZEPP: Jah. [*He puts on coat and hat*]

KATE: Now, Menno, you promised, remember?

MENNO: I said I'll do what I can, Katie.

KATE: Menno, please.

ZEPP: Just let me do the talking.

MENNO: I can't go against my conscience. Not even for you.

[MENNO *and* ZEPP *exit.*]

LYDIE: Come and get warm, Katie. There's coffee yet.

[KATE *goes to the stove to warm her hands and pours coffee.*]

LYDIE: I'm surprised to see you out. Menno said you weren't feeling well? [*Fishing*]

KATE: I think it was just a touch of the flu.

LYDIE: [*Disappointed*] Oh, are you sure?

KATE: Where's Martha?

LYDIE: I sent her over to give Susan Meyer a hand. They've got it bad, both of them.

KATE: Susan's mother won't even talk to her since they switched to East Zorra.

LYDIE: I know. And she don't have many friends in her new church yet. You don't want strangers when you're miserable. Have you seen the baby? [*Giggles*] It's got Rube's ears.

KATE: Jah, I'm glad you're letting Martha help out.

LYDIE: Even Christy wouldn't say the ban keeps us from looking after the sick.

KATE: Christy can be so hateful and hard to please. And then he smiles at you and you feel that safe.

LYDIE: I wish you'd known him when he was young ... He ... oh, never mind. It's all gone now. Tell me what you're doing to your house?

KATE: Menno managed to get the kitchen finished, and we can make do with one bedroom.

LYDIE: For awhile.

KATE: Jah. Trouble is, he's going to all these meetings down in Baden.

LYDIE: He's not getting mixed up in politics, too?

KATE: Jah, and how can I complain about not having my house fixed up when there's all these Mennonites coming out of Russia and our government not letting them in? Oh, it's those high people and their stupid laws.

LYDIE: We were so sure the bad feeling would go after the war ended. At least Mrs. O'Rourke is back to normal.

KATE: Have you talked to the Devil again?

LYDIE: You'll never guess what they have now.

KATE: What?

LYDIE: A piano. She let me play it.

KATE: You know how?

LYDIE: I played a whole tune.

KATE: I thought you had to take lessons for years.

LYDIE: Oh, I guess the·high people are that fond of school they make up something hard about it. You just sit there and pump your feet and them little white things go up and down by themselves.

KATE: Maybe it's the Devil hiding inside. [*They laugh*]

LYDIE: [*Sadly*] I miss Hannah that much.

KATE: Me, too.

LYDIE: Christy is just lost without her.

[MENNO *and* ZEPP *enter* CHRISTY*'s kitchen.*]

CHRISTY: What are you doing here?

ZEPP: The three of us are going to get agreement.

[ZEPP *sits.*]

CHRISTY: Your son-in-law is destroying my father's church and you bring him over here like this was some dispute over fences?

ZEPP: Sit down.

[MENNO *and* CHRISTY *sit. It is evident* CHRISTY *has been drinking.*]

CHRISTY: I'm not backing down, Zepp. Either he submits or I'm putting him out.

ZEPP: Now, he took the lightning rod off his barn. He put the old kind of top back on his buggy, and he told Rube Meyer he wouldn't go in on that tractor.

CHRISTY: [*Surprised*] He still has to get up and say he repents his sins.

MENNO: Well, I ... sins is ...

ZEPP: Maybe he could say that he's sorry he got in conflict with the bishop.

MENNO: [*This is hard to swallow*] Jah ... I ...

CHRISTY: No. He has to admit them things are sinful.

[ZEPP *looks at* MENNO, *who shakes his head.*]

ZEPP: Suppose he said squabbling over them was sinful.

CHRISTY: Wanting them.

ZEPP: Wanting them — too much.

CHRISTY: Jah.

MENNO: Jah. [*Pause*]

ZEPP: How sweet it is for brethren to dwell together in unity.

CHRISTY: There's that Sunday school.

MENNO: I talked to the crowd and —

ZEPP: They all promise not to allow one word except it be German. They'll stick right to the Bible and they'll stop four-part singing.

CHRISTY: They'll stop the whole thing.

MENNO: But that's all the congregation —

ZEPP: As far as I recall, Christy, the congregation didn't ask for more than that.

CHRISTY: We never had to postpone communion in this church before.

ZEPP: Jah, but —

CHRISTY: In all the years we been a congregation, not once did we fail to get enough agreement to say we were at peace.

ZEPP: I know.

CHRISTY: Every one of the dissenting votes was from a Sunday schooler.

ZEPP: Well, jah ...

CHRISTY: And of them that quit, how many were Sunday school-ers?

ZEPP: Well ...

CHRISTY: All of them, Deacon.

ZEPP: I'll grant you that, but ...

CHRISTY: Will you grant me that if I put a stop to their study meeting, I'll put an end to what's ripping my church apart?

MENNO: No! You'll put a stop to the only thing that's keeping the rest of us in. If you'd just come and see the work we're doing —

CHRISTY: I see the fruits. You pore over the Bible, not for comfort, not for wisdom. No, you're looking for ways to put your elders in the wrong. You take a couple of words out of a verse, you twist them all around so you can justify any fancy things you want.

MENNO: No. So we can carry on Christ's ministry instead of hiding our light.

CHRISTY: You multiply words without knowledge. You think our fathers were fools.

ZEPP: Now, just a minute ...

CHRISTY: You think your bishop is a fool. You better remember one verse that's pretty clear. 'Rebellion is as the sin of witchcraft.' And stubbornness is as iniquity and idolatry.

MENNO: Against God, yes. But you're making a golden calf out of tradition. And I'm not going to bow down to it.

ZEPP: To obey is better than to sacrifice, Menno.

MENNO: Obey who? A bishop that's drunk as Balcassar and proud as Nebucarnesser?

ZEPP: Enough.

MENNO: It's him who's driving us out. Just like he drove out his son.

[*Silence.*]

CHRISTY: Get out of my house.

MENNO: I'm sorry, I —

ZEPP: Go on home, Menno.

MENNO: Zepp, I —

ZEPP: I'll be along in a bit. Go on. [MENNO *exits*]

[CHRISTY *pours himself a glass of wine.*]

ZEPP: Friendly, aren't you?

CHRISTY: Go home and leave me in peace.

ZEPP: Peace, is it? [*Silence*] Why don't you let me send one of the girls over to clean this place up? [*Picks up jug*] This what you had for supper? [*Pours himself one*] You got to allow, Christy, 'Whatever kind of words you speak, the like you shall hear.'

[*Silence.*]

ZEPP: We already lost six members to East Zorra. If Menno goes, more are going to follow. [*Silence*] Christy, if we have a split, it's not going to be like when your father took a few families and we started meeting together. This is neighbour against neighbour, father against son.

CHRISTY: I want to keep my father's church pure.

ZEPP: It's our church.

CHRISTY: I'm bishop.

ZEPP: Jah. [*Pause*] Christy, I've never gone against you, not once in all the years we've known each other.

CHRISTY: You want to quit being deacon.

ZEPP: No. And I don't want to switch membership either, but you go on like this, and I might have to stand against you.

CHRISTY: You think it was me!

ZEPP: What?

CHRISTY: You blame me for my son being a killer!

ZEPP: What are you talking about?

CHRISTY: Where do you think he got the idea from? They talked about the war at those meetings.

ZEPP: You're not making sense.

CHRISTY: That Bible group. He writes to them ... did you know that?

ZEPP: You mean Yock?

CHRISTY: I never drove him out. They're lying.

ZEPP: Menno shouldn't have said that ...

CHRISTY: They say I was too hard on him, because of her. Well, it's not true. I knew it wasn't his fault, her dying like that.

ZEPP: Christy...

CHRISTY: I tried to make it up to him ... that's where I went wrong ... I was too easy ... I spared him too much ... But I'm not making the same mistake with the church.

ZEPP: That isn't what all this is about, is it? Are we going to be split from our children because you couldn't keep your son at home?

CHRISTY: They've got a choice ... like he had a choice ... and if they want to say I drove them out, then we're well rid of them, like I'm well rid of him.

ZEPP: You're the one that has a choice, Christy. Folks aren't against you because of what Yock did, they're against you because you treat the church the same way you treated him. No one's blaming you near as much as you're blaming yourself. You've let your grief ruin your life, and now you're letting your pride ruin ours.

CHRISTY: You telling me I'm proud?

ZEPP: You wanted to be Bishop. Your father was, so you had to be. And you're too proud to allow you might have failed a bit. With Yock. With all of us.

[ZEPP *exits.* CHRISTY *sits down with his Bible.*]

CHRISTY: 'Seekest thou great things for thyself, seek them not.'

[CHRISTY *opens the Bible and begins to read.*]

[KATE *puts down her handiwork and goes to the stove.*]

KATE: Do you want some more coffee, Mom?

LYDIE: No, thanks.

KATE: You can stop looking at me like that. I'm not pregnant.

LYDIE: Oh, Katie.

KATE: Oh, Mom, it's just ...

LYDIE: You want a child that much?

KATE: What else did I get married for?

LYDIE: Give yourself time, it's not even a year yet.

KATE: The house is so lonely, though ... and now if we have to leave the church ...

LYDIE: Your doddy won't let that happen.

KATE: I married Menno so we could all stay together, you know.

LYDIE: I know.

KATE: Mom, I have to tell you something. This evening I was looking out of the window. Watching the snow drifts. I saw a man at the bottom of our lane, just standing there, staring up at the house. He didn't move. He just stood there till he was covered with snow. Mom, I think it was Yock.

LYDIE: You're seeing things.

KATE: I had to grab on to the chair to keep from running out screaming his name.

LYDIE: Katie, pull yourself together. You've got a good man. You'll have children. Kate, believe me, in time you'll forget you ever wanted anything else.

Kate Trotter (Kate) and Janet Amos (Lydie).

KATE: No, no, Mom. I love him. That's why I came over tonight. I was afraid to stay by myself. Mom, if he comes back, if he ...

[*Knock at the door.* MENNO *enters.*]

LYDIE: [*Flustered*] Menno, what are you knocking for?

[KATE *turns away to regain her composure.*]

MENNO: Oh, well. [*Pause*] Are you ready to go, Kate?

KATE: You didn't get agreement.

MENNO: Kate, the Lord asks some hard things sometimes.

KATE: The Lord asks. [*Bitter*]

MENNO: I'm switching to East Zorra. Christy's putting me out. [*Pause*] Katie, I don't think anyone would blame you for staying.

LYDIE: [*Shocked*] Now, Kate, you don't think we would ever turn our backs on you, do you?

KATE: [*Going to her*] Would you and doddy switch, too? You never thought Christy should be bishop.

LYDIE: But he is. And we won't turn our backs on him neither.

KATE: You could have a telephone. And a piano maybe.

LYDIE: Ach, Katie, you're not as silly as that. I only want them things on the outside. The church is on the inside. All them things are just what might be nice, like summer all year 'round. But you have to understand, it's different for your man. Here's your shawl. Put your bonnet on tight now.

MENNO: Kate?

[KATE *ties her bonnet and she and* MENNO *exit.*]

[LYDIE *tidies up a bit, worried and sad.* ZEPP *enters.*]

LYDIE: Zepp, I'm worried to death.

ZEPP: Menno told you?

LYDIE: Jah.

ZEPP: I can't halt between two opinions anymore.

LYDIE: It's going to kill Katie ... I mean it, Zepp.

ZEPP: Remember that fuss they had over in Wilmot a couple of years ago?

LYDIE: [*Impatient*] No.

ZEPP: They deposed a bishop. For lording it over his flock.

LYDIE: Can you do that?

ZEPP: We'd have to find another bishop to put it to the congregation. [*Pause*] Eli Frey is back. Visiting in East Zorra. [ZEPP *puts his hat back on and exits*]

[*Blackout*]

scene iv
The exterior of the Bauman house
The next morning, early

YOCK approaches CHRISTY's door. CHRISTY is sitting inside. The oil lamp may still be lit.

YOCK is dressed as any demobbed soldier and carries a bag. He hesitates, then knocks on the door. There is no response. He knocks again. CHRISTY opens the door a crack.

YOCK: Pa, it's me. I've come home.

[CHRISTY *slams the door shut.*]

YOCK: [*Knocking*] Pa, please open the door. [YOCK *tries the handle,* CHRISTY *holds it shut*] Pa!

[CHRISTY *bolts the door from the inside.*]

YOCK: Pa ... let me in. [*He pounds on the door*] Please let me in. [*Pause*] Grosmutti, Grosmutti, are you there?

CHRISTY: Go away... leave me alone.

YOCK: Pa, I have to talk to you ... I have to. Open the door. [*Rattles door*] Open it! I been half way 'round the world and I've come back. I've come to tell you something and you're going to listen. You never listened to me in your life, did you? Well, listen now. I killed a man. Do you hear me, Pa? I killed a man. They tell me I killed more, but there was only one I ever saw. We were going up this hill and he came at me. I stuck out my bayonet like it was my arm, and I got him in the gut. He was lying in the mud, screaming and bleeding. Everybody else kept going on, but I just stood there shaking. He was going to die right there in that mud and he knew it. He was afraid, Pa. He was afraid of facing God. He started screaming for a preacher. I wanted to tell him I understood, that I was Christian, that I was German, too. I wanted to say all those words I used to hear you read from the Bible, but I was ashamed. So I let him die like that in the mud. That was the war, Pa. That's what it was. You know, I thought I was going off to save you all from something. I bet he did, too. I thought the King of England was going to be there like in the school books, cheering me on. Somehow I even thought I was going to put the legs back on Paddy O'Rourke. But all I did was put a knife into a man ... and Pa, he looked like Zepp. If he'd had a beard, he could have been Zepp. And right at the end, he cried out for his father to come and take him home, and I started crying for you. I wanted you to come over the hill and take me home. Because I knew, if I'd just stayed home ... I guess that's what I ... what I wanted to tell you, Pa ... If I'd just stayed. I'm going away now. You don't have to worry. I'll keep out of your way ...

[YOCK *picks up his bag.*]

[KATE *enters. She stops when she sees* YOCK.]

KATE: It was you. Yock, it was you.

YOCK: Katie ... [*He goes to her*]

KATE: They said I was seeing things ... but I knew ...

YOCK: Oh, Katie ... [THEY *embrace*] Just let me hold you. Please, just let me hold you.

KATE: There's straw in your hair.

YOCK: I slept in the barn.

KATE: Yock, why?

YOCK: I had to work my courage up.

KATE: I suppose you haven't had anything to eat?

YOCK: Real little Amish woman. [*Pause*] Kate, I was a soldier ...

KATE: I don't care. As long as you're back ... as long as you're safe, I don't care what you did.

YOCK: Do you mean that? You don't know how much I hoped someone would say that to me. [*He hugs her*] It's all right. Everything will be all right ... somehow ...

KATE: Oh, Yock ...

YOCK: Don't cry. I'm home and I'll find some way ... If I could just talk to Grosmutti ... [KATE *draws away*] What's wrong?

KATE: Did you think you could come home, and find nothing changed?

YOCK: [*Pause*] When?

KATE: Last summer.

YOCK: [*Pause*] I wrote to Menno, you know. But I never heard anything back.

KATE: Why didn't you write to me?

YOCK: Your folks would have seen the letter.

KATE: But I would have known you were coming home!

YOCK: I didn't know myself. I thought I was clear of here for good. It wasn't until I got out of hospital –

KATE: Were you wounded?

YOCK: No, they said it was fatigue or something. I couldn't stop shaking. When I got better I tried to wander around, see the world for a bit ... but I knew I had to face things ... I guess. I couldn't just leave it with me running off like that.

KATE: I wish I had gone with you that night.

YOCK: No ... I didn't know where I was going or why ... But it's different now, Kate ... I mean ... it's not too late. Even if they won't take me back, I could find another church. There must be one that'll take a repentant sinner ... one who's willing to tell silly young boys how well off they are.

KATE: Don't joke about it.

YOCK: I'm not joking. I got to make some good out of all this. But, Kate, it won't be here, I'd just embarrass Pa ... maybe close, though ... visiting distance ... Would you ... I mean, I passed by the Stutzman farm last night ... There's folks living there ... and I thought ... it could have been me and you ...

KATE: Yock, don't you know?

YOCK: What?

KATE: That's my house. I saw you in the lane ... no, of course you don't know.

YOCK: What is it?

KATE: I got married. I married Menno.

[*Silence.*]

YOCK: [*Harshly*] Why did you come here?

KATE: I had to see you. I couldn't ... They told me you'd never come back.

YOCK: Does your man know you're here?

KATE: Did you think I'd spend my whole life waiting?

YOCK: When I turned around and you were standing there ... I thought it was a sign that God had forgiven me. Go home, Kate. Go home. [*Seeing her unhappiness*] Oh, Katie, oh God, no.

[YOCK *takes* KATE *in his arms.* LYDIE, ZEPP *and* MENNO *enter.* KATE *breaks from* YOCK *but remains near him.*]

LYDIE: Katie, you scared us half to death ... Menno came and told us he woke up and you weren't there.

MENNO: Kate, it's not me and him you have to choose between. I know there wouldn't be much of a choice for you then. It's him and the Christian life.

KATE: I never meant to hurt you.

MENNO: I never meant to hurt you, either. But we are married. If it weren't for that, I wouldn't try to stop you. I'm going back to the house now, and when you come, I'll understand. I mean, I won't bother you or nothing. Or hold a grudge. I love you, you know, but I guess that don't interest you much. [*He turns to leave*]

YOCK: Menno ...

[MENNO *does not turn around but exits.* CHRISTY *comes out having seen* MENNO *leave without* KATE.]

CHRISTY: [*To* YOCK] There's nothing between you and her anymore.

YOCK: I know. Pa, are you all right?

KATE: Christy, you thought he was dead to us. And he's home. I've got no choice left, but you do. You can leave him damned or you can help him. and if you turn your back on him now, I'm leaving the church. And I'm not just switching my membership, I'm clearing right out. Because the church is supposed to be about love, and it's not.

CHRISTY: Kate ...

YOCK: Lydie, take her home.

KATE: I'll go myself. Mom, at least see he gets fed.

[KATE *begins to walk off.* LYDIE *stops her.*]

LYDIE: [*To* CHRISTY] Christy, that is Sarah's child.

CHRISTY: I know that.

YOCK: [*Picking up bags*] I'm not going to bother anyone anymore.

ZEPP: You're welcome to come home with me, Yock.

YOCK: No. [*He starts off*]

CHRISTY: Yock ...

[YOCK *and* CHRISTY *look at each other. Silence.*]

KATE: Please, Christy ...

CHRISTY: It's not that I'm leaving you damned ...

YOCK: Pa, did I do this to you? [*Pause*] Pa, listen to me ...

CHRISTY: I heard ...

YOCK: I came home to tell you you were right ... You were right all along.

Janet Amos (Lydie) and Kate Trotter (Kate).

CHRISTY: You ... you can be saved ... you just ... you can't ...

YOCK: I understand, Pa. This isn't my home anymore. [*To* KATE] I'm sorry, Katie ... I'm sorry you ever laid eyes on me.

CHRISTY: If you need ... what are you going to do?

YOCK: I'll be all right. I still have my soldier's pay.

[YOCK *exits.*]

ZEPP: Go after him.

CHRISTY: He isn't one of us anymore.

LYDIE: Sarah gave her life for Yock ...

CHRISTY: I know.

LYDIE: Because she thought you wanted him.

CHRISTY: I did. [*Pause*] Isn't wanting a funny thing? Wanting a son cost me my wife. Once I had him, all I wanted was her. Now, wanting to keep the church safe has cost me my son. And I never wanted him as much as I do this minute.

KATE: You can't just let him go.

CHRISTY: Katie, it isn't a question of letting. He touched the unclean thing, and it touched him. The mark of Cain is upon him. He isn't one of us anymore ... couldn't you see that? But the Lord will look after him for us. You have your own life.

[KATE *begins to walk off.*]

LYDIE: Kate, believe me, in time ...

KATE: Jah, I know.

[KATE *exits.* ZEPP *indicates to* LYDIE *that she is to leave.* LYDIE *exits. Silence between* ZEPP *and* CHRISTY.]

CHRISTY: She didn't mean that, not about clearing out.

ZEPP: Well, if you force a split, she won't mind switching.

CHRISTY: [*Pause*] He told me I was right.

ZEPP: I heard.

Beth Amos (Hannah) and Rachel Thompson (child).

CHRISTY: I wasn't sure ... inspite of what I been saying ... I wasn't sure of anything at all ... not until I saw him again. [*Pause*] But now I know Menno's wrong, Zepp. When you came over last night, I said we weren't having a dispute over fences ... but that's just what it is, Zepp. That's why my father's rules are right. I never understood before, not clearly. Working the land the old way, the women's covering's ... all those little traditions that Menno calls the golden calf ... they won't buy our salvation, but those are our fences. And they're not there to keep us in, you know. What they do is keep the wolves from coming in and tearing out our hearts, like they tore out Yock's.

ZEPP: [*Pause*] You'd better know, I was over in East Zorra. Eli Frey is coming Sunday.

CHRISTY: You didn't waste any time. [*Pause*] Well, I won't say you didn't have cause, maybe I shouldn't go on being bishop. [*Pause*] All right, Zepp, let Eli come and have his say. But I'm still going to have mine. I'm not going to let Menno Miller or any other foolish sheep go tearing down those fences and letting the wolves in, at least not until they hear from me what happened to my son. Then as to whether we split or whether they overthrow me as bishop, well, I'll leave that to the members and to the Lord.

ZEPP: Christy, you're doing the right thing.

[ZEPP *exits.*]

[CHRISTY *goes to his door and stands a moment looking in the direction* YOCK *has gone.*]

[*Blackout*]

Author's Notes

THE COMMUNITY

The Amish community described in *Quiet in the Land* is loosely derived from a number of congregations that existed in 1917, but it is not modeled on any particular one. Each church (note that church always refers to the community of Christians and never to a building) had its own individual character within a general tradition because specific rules or responses to particular situations were decided by consensus of the membership rather than by a central authority. The churches were small in order to maintain a strongly cohesive unit and so that all members could travel from their farms to a meeting conveniently. If the population grew too large a new group would be formed. Similarly a new church could arise from a difference of opinion within the original membership. Often this was accomplished without animosity; when disputes did become hostile it was usually due to the personal failings of strong-minded leaders.

BISHOP ELI FREY

Eli Frey is the only character in the play who is not fictional. He did have 'oversight' of a few churches in Waterloo County that were too small to have a bishop of their own. This oversight was interrupted by the war and his difficulties with the border guards are documented. Frey belonged to the progressive element in the church and worked to bring the Amish to a General Conference that would achieve greater unity within the Anabaptist family. However, he did not succeed until 1922.

THE CLERGY

Usually each church had a bishop, a minister (preacher) and a deacon. When the need arose to fill one of these positions the membership would nominate men from among themselves. If there were a number of nominations, the selection would be made by drawing lots, so that the final choice would be 'left to the lord'. The duties of the deacon included maintaining discipline on a day-to-day basis and settling any disputes or differences with the membership. The clergy received no financial support at this time and carried on farming like everybody else. Although they had authority within the church, they were expected to act in accordance with the wishes of the membership and major decisions were taken by the church as a whole.

SUNDAY WORSHIP

Most of the Amish in 1917 met in plain white meeting houses, but there were a minority who still preferred the practice of meeting in homes. The community in *Quiet in the Land* belongs to this group to facilitate staging. If the opportunity to provide a meeting house in some future production were to arise, there would be no loss of accuracy; however as this community is conservative they would not be unlikely to meet in homes. Each family took its turn in hosting a meeting, and all the women helped in the preparation of the meal that followed.

THE CHARACTERS

The Amish of this play are simply farmers of German origin whose lives are shaped by a certainty of religious belief that seems foreign in today's society. They are not an alien species or a mystical cult. They are neither dour nor puritanical in their day-to-day activities. Like other farm families, they enjoy great quantities of home-produced food prepared in a German style, and the centre of home life is the kitchen table. They do not use two words where one will do, but they enjoy a joke, laugh a great deal and love to quote 'sayings' of which they have an enormous number. Members of an Old Order Community such as this one usually prefer to keep to themselves but they are not shy, self-conscious or self-righteous when dealing with outsiders.

BAPTISM

Boys and girls are usually baptised between the ages of 16 and 20. A candidate for baptism takes classes for a number of weeks prior to being received into the church. With baptism comes full church membership and all the duties and privileges of adulthood including the right to begin courting. The form of baptism (which is included in some productions of the play where the scene is visible behind the YOCK — PADDY scene) is:

[KATE *and* MENNO *leave their places and kneel before the* BISHOP. ZEPP *(the Deacon) stands beside the* BISHOP *with a small jug of water.* LYDIE *(in the absence of the* BISHOP's *wife who would normally perform this function) removes* KATE's *bonnet and covering.*]

BISHOP: Wherefore come you out from among them and be ye separate and touch not the unclean thing, and I will receive you, saith the lord.

[*The* BISHOP *cups his hands over* MENNO's *head.* ZEPP *pours a small quantity of water into the* BISHOP's *hands.*]

BISHOP: On confession of your faith, repenting and grieving of your sins, you are baptised in the Name of the Father, Son and Holy Ghost. [*He releases a few drops of water on each name of the Trinity. He turns to* KATE, *the action is repeated.*] In the Name of the Father, Son and Holy Ghost. [*He turns back to* MENNO] Be welcome as a brother in the church. [BISHOP *raises* MENNO *and gives him the kiss of peace.*]

[LYDIE *raises* KATE *and kisses her, and replaces the 'covering' on her head.*]

SOCIAL LIFE

As with most farmers of the period, much of the Amish social life revolved around work in form of 'bees', such as barn-raising, quilting and corn shucking. The corn shucking scene in this play has been modified for the stage. It would have occurred in the field with stacks of field corn being prepared to feed the livestock. Such little traditions as red ears providing a chance to kiss are shared with many agricultural societies. For a production where corn is not available, apple schnitzing (peeling, paring and stringing in preparation for drying) could be substituted. Perhaps worms could provide an instant traditional kiss.

Learning the difficult hymns, which were never written down, was also turned into a social occasion. Accomplished singers would teach the young people the hymns at 'singings', usually held at someone's home on a Sunday evening. This was where the younger members of the community got together without too many of the older generation, and often where courting began.

At any of these functions, wholesome fun was quite in order. Board games were popular. And although dancing was forbidden, the idea that homemade wines, cordials, or tobacco in moderation were sinful belonged to the progressive or evangelical element. The great sin for the Old Order was any display of pride of possession or knowledge, 'thinking you were better than anybody else'. Titles, including Mr. and Mrs., were considered 'worldly' so that even young children would address older people by their first names.

COURTING

Early marriages were encouraged; however the choice of partner (within the community) was left to the young people. Parents did not interfere overtly. The 'dating' practices were liberal by Victorian standards with private visiting and buggy riding allowed. There was a tradition for the courting couple to keep a serious relationship secret until the bans were announced by the Deacon at Sunday meeting. If everyone was surprised, the couple enjoyed a little triumph. Finding out who was serious about whom was therefore a challenge enjoyed by everyone else.

SET AND COSTUME DESIGN
The interior of Amish houses was marked by simplicity, order and a plain scrubbed look. Colour was provided by quilts, cushions and rag rugs, but nothing of a purely ornamental nature would be found anywhere.

The costume designers of *Quiet in the Land* are able to choose from a variety of specific practices within a general tradition. The 'plain coat', a particular style of black suit for baptised men, was common to all, as was the practice of using hooks and eyes, and braces rather than buttons or belts which were considered to be of military origin. Short hair for men was also considered too military, as were moustaches. The women wore prayer caps or 'coverings' at all times, but there is some variation as to whether the strings are black or white, and in whether they are tied under the chin or hang loosely over the chest. How much hair, if any, can be shown at the front can also be left to the designer. Whatever decisions are made, the important thing is that each character observes the same dress code. There would be no personal choices within the community. The apron is part of the women's outfit and appears to be derived from the medieval style of dress, as are the habits of certain orders of nuns. In everyday wear, the aprons and dresses may be of solid darker colours that suggest home dying, and the apron need not be of the same fabric or colour. However, for formal occasions and church, the baptised women wear black dresses and aprons. Whether the children wear formal blacks may be left to the designer and the budget. Periwinkle blue appears to be the most popular colour for the bride. Her apron might be white, but not the dress. Men's shirts can be from the same dye vat as the women's dresses. Their pants are almost always black. The traditional black hat is for church and winter. Straw hats are used in summer. The Bishop, and in some congregations, the Deacon, wear a special caped coat.

MUSIC
The Amish hymns resemble Gregorian chant. There is no accompaniment and no harmony. The 'vorsinger' (always a man in church, but

on social occasions a woman or girl could lead) sings the first few notes and controls the melody. The hymn book used by the Old Order at this time was the Ausbund. It has the lyrics in High German but no notes. Music was not written down, but passed orally through the generations. The music used in the original production of *Quiet in the Land* can be obtained through the author.

LANGUAGE

Among themselves the Amish speak a low German dialect into which many foreign phrases have been introduced. In this play it is translated into the ordinary speech of rural Ontario. High German was used for church, so the hymns are not translated. I have used a convention that when the Amish are speaking English, as in the scenes with O'Rourke and the Recruiting officer, they speak with accents. As the children were allowed to attend ordinary school until the legal school leaving age (14) their English is more fluent than that of the adults. The English language was looked upon as 'proud and worldly', and once the children had left school, they would not have spoken it again except under necessity. The only books in the home would be a German Bible and the Martyr's Mirror (a history of Mennonite persecutions in gory detail). There were some German publications, mostly news of relatives and a sermon or inspirational message, published in Ohio, but these were not permitted across the border in war time.

CONSCRIPTION AND THE MENNONITE EXCLUSION

There was considerable legal confusion about the status of the non-resistant sects during the war. The law was ambiguous and its application was not consistent. Newspapers of the time show very clearly the antipathy of the general population to German-speaking pacifists and, after the war, such emigrants, including the refugees from the Russian revolution, were not admitted to Canada.

Anne Chislett was born in St. John's, Newfoundland, in 1942. She graduated with a B.A. (Hons. English) from Memorial University in 1964 and went on to graduate studies in theatre at the University of British Columbia. Following a brief career teaching English and theatre in Ontario high schools, she assisted her husband, James Roy, in founding the Blyth Summer Festival in 1975. Her first play, *A Summer Burning,* adapted from the novel of Harry J. Boyle, was produced there in 1977. She remained in theatre administration at Blyth and Theatre Passe Muraille until 1980 when the success of her second play *The Tomorrow Box,* first produced at Kawartha Summer Theatre, enabled her to make playwriting a full-time occupation. She received the 1982 Chalmers Canadian Play Award for *Quiet in the Land* following its production at Toronto Free Theatre. Ms. Chislett now resides in Victoria, B.C.

Other drama titles available from
COACH HOUSE PRESS

Making, Out: Plays by Gay Men

Edited and with an Introduction by ROBERT WALLACE.
DAVID DEMCHUK, KEN GARNHUM, SKY GILBERT,
DANIEL MACIVOR, HARRY RINTOUL, COLIN THOMAS
Six bold new plays—ranging from Gilbert's "very gay little
musical" *Capote at Yaddo* to Thomas's moving study of the effect
of AIDS in *Flesh and Blood*—map the terrain of contemporary
gay male culture and challenge the perimeters of Canadian
society.

The Noam Chomsky Lectures

DANIEL BROOKS AND GUILLERMO VERDECCHIA
This meta-theatrical explication of the teachings of cultural
theorist Noam Chomsky won a 1991 Chalmers Award for Outstanding New Play. "A fine introduction to thinking critically
about the interpenetrations of media, business and government:
a sort of Intellectual Self-Defence 101." — *Quill & Quire*

Goodnight Desdemona (Good Morning Juliet)

ANN-MARIE MACDONALD
Winner of the 1990 Governor General's Award for Drama.
Goodnight Desdemona is "one of the wildest and woolliest feminist
reappraisals [of Shakespeare's heroines] that the theatre has
recently seen, and one of the most intellectually ambitious."
— Ray Conlogue, *The Globe and Mail*

Lilies: Or The Revival of a Romantic Drama

MICHEL MARC BOUCHARD
"The most powerful play to emerge from Quebec in many years.
Its language, inspired by Pre-Raphaelite paintings, is full of the
plumage of youthful beauty and of exalted emotions that can
never quite have existed. Bouchard's script lives up to its magnificent effrontery." — Ray Conlogue, *The Globe and Mail*

Other drama titles available from
COACH HOUSE PRESS

Lion in the Streets
JUDITH THOMPSON

Isobel, a young Portuguese girl who was brutally murdered seventeen years before the play begins, returns to her neighbourhood to find her killer. Judith Thompson "has the power...not merely to imagine characters at the extreme edges of experience, but to voice them." — Robert Nunn, *Canadian Theatre Review*

The Other Side of the Dark
JUDITH THOMPSON

Winner of the 1989 Governor General's Award for Drama, this volume includes Thompson's most-acclaimed play, *The Crackwalker*, as well as *I Am Yours*, *Pink*, and *Tornado*. "Thompson is a powerful and original voice in Canadian theatre." — Robert Crew, *The Toronto Star*

Bag Babies: A Comedy of (Bad) Manners
ALLAN STRATTON

Nominated for the 1991 City of Toronto Book Award. "A brilliant, funny satire about urban hunger and homelessness, about the parvenu rich, about the wretched pomposity of the news media and 'greed without guilt.' [This is] theatre very much at the centre of life." — Michael Valpy, *The Globe and Mail*

Words in Play: Three Comedies
ALLAN STRATTON

"Stratton's genius is in taking everyday situations and — like Molière — giving them the right kind of comic or bizarre twist to make us notice the real issue driving the plot: the struggle between good and evil or illusion and reality, and the foibles of human beings revealed in the struggle to cope." — *Literature and Language*

Other drama titles available from
COACH HOUSE PRESS

The Book of Jessica
LINDA GRIFFITHS AND MARIA CAMPBELL
"A fascinating study not only of the tortuous birth of a magnificent play but of the relationship of two women driven apart and bound together by a maelstrom of internal and external forces."
— Janet Silman, *The Globe and Mail*

Willful Acts
MARGARET HOLLINGSWORTH
"Women and their relationships, both with each other and with men, is the topic of the five Hollingsworth plays gathered in *Willful Acts*. They are all tantalizing pieces of theatre." — *Now Magazine*

The End / A Day at the Beach
JOHN PALMER
The End: "A fiendishly organized, accelerating farce, worked out with brilliant dexterity." — Urjo Kareda, *The Globe and Mail* • *A Day at the Beach:* "The most capable and deeply expressed treatment of gay themes I've seen for a long, long time." — Dayne Ogilvie, *Extra!*

Farther West / New World
JOHN MURRELL
Winner of the Floyd S. Chalmers and Canadian Authors Association Best Play awards. "Murrell's dramatic landscape...emphasizes women as creators of their own rules and environments."
— Martin Knelman, *Saturday Night*

Other drama titles available from
COACH HOUSE PRESS

Escape from Happiness
GEORGE F. WALKER
The large, fractured family of Walker's East End Trilogy finds
harmony amidst the chaos of bungled police, criminal and
vigilante activities. "The best thing about the play is Walker's use
of language, for he creates his own universe with it, using speech
rhythms that change gears unexpectedly, in blips and eccentric
dialogue that rides the edge of the familiar into the absurd."
— Liam Lacey, *The Globe and Mail*

Love and Anger
GEORGE F. WALKER
Winner of a Chalmers Outstanding New Play Award. Renegade
lawyer Petie Maxwell takes on the forces of greed and corruption
in the person of tabloid owner Babe Conner, one of the power
brokers bent on turning the city into a place that is only satisfying
for baseball fans and real estate agents. "Walker's writing is tauter
and tougher than ever. *Love And Anger* is a triumph, a fiercely
comic flowering of a major and mature talent."
— Doug Bale, *London Free Press*

Nothing Sacred
GEORGE F. WALKER
Winner of the 1988 Governor General's Award for Drama.
"Russian writer Ivan Turgenev first popularized the term 'nihilist'
in his great 1862 novel *Fathers and Sons*, one of the most vivid
creations of Russian literature. In *Nothing Sacred*, Walker has
caught the novel's broad sympathies and subtle play of ideas in
a brilliant stage version. Although he amplifies the gentle hum-
our of Turgenev's tragicomedy to near-farcical levels, the result
is spell-binding." — John Bemrose, *Maclean's*

Other drama titles available from
COACH HOUSE PRESS

The Power Plays
GEORGE F. WALKER
Investigator T.M. Power and his sidekick do battle with the corrupt and capricious, decadent and desperate, rich and famous, and makers and breakers of culture and control in this trilogy of comic thriller plays, *Gossip*, *Filthy Rich* and *The Art of War*.

Three Plays
GEORGE F. WALKER
Walker's unerring eye for detail and his ability to combine these details into a world at once mysterious and comedic are brilliantly displayed in *Bagdad Saloon*, *Beyond Mozambique* and *Ramona and the White Slaves*.

Seen through the Press by Robert Wallace
Typeset in Bembo and printed in Canada

THE COACH HOUSE PRESS
401 (rear) Huron Street
Toronto, Canada M 5S 2G 5